**W9-ANX-472**

# New Jersey

# NEW JERSEY
# BY ROAD

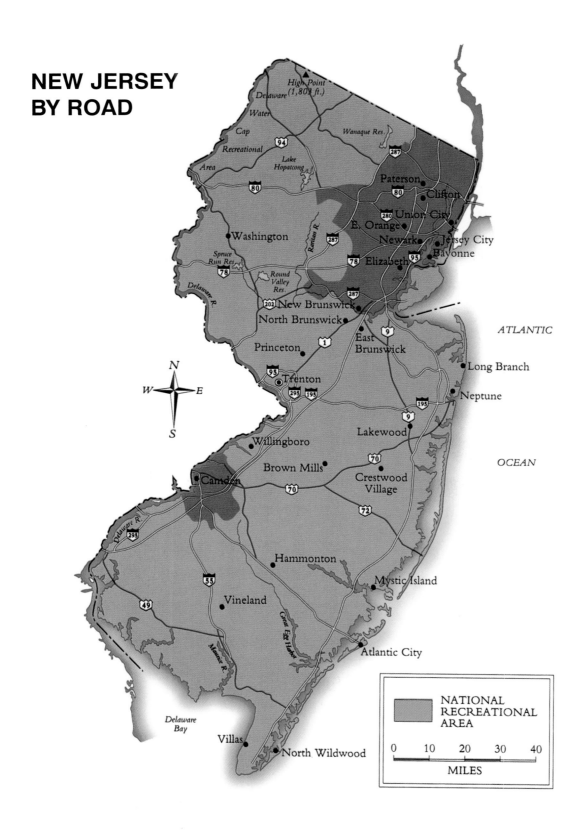

High Point
(1,803 ft.)

Delaware

Water

Cap

Recreational

Area

Wanaque Res.

94

Lake
Hopatcong

Raritan R.

80

287

Paterson

80

Clifton

280 Union City

E. Orange

Newark

Jersey City
Bayonne

78

Elizabeth

95

Washington

Spruce
Run Res.

78

Round
Valley
Res.

287

Delaware R.

203 New Brunswick

North Brunswick

287

Princeton

1

East
Brunswick

9

ATLANTIC

95 Trenton

295 195

Long Branch

Neptune

195

9

Lakewood

OCEAN

Willingboro

70

Brown Mills

Crestwood
Village

Camden

70

72

Delaware R.

295

Hammonton

55

Mystic Island

49

Vineland

Great Egg Harbor

Maurice R.

Atlantic City

Delaware
Bay

Villas

North Wildwood

N

W          E

S

NATIONAL
RECREATIONAL
AREA

0    10    20    30    40

MILES

## Celebrate the States

# New Jersey

## Wendy Moragne and Tamra B. Orr

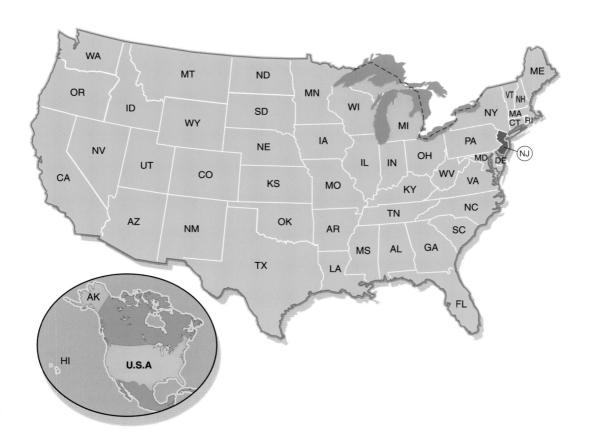

Marshall Cavendish
Benchmark
New York

Marshall Cavendish Benchmark
99 White Plains Road
Tarrytown, NY 10591-5502
www.marshallcavendish.us

All Internet sites were correct at time of printing.

Library of Congress Cataloging-in-Publication Data
Moragne, Wendy.
New Jersey / by Wendy Moragne and Tamra B. Orr. — 2nd ed.
p. cm. — (Celebrate the states)
Summary: "Provides comprehensive information on the geography, history, wildlife, governmental
structure, economy, cultural diversity, peoples, religion, and landmarks of
New Jersey"—Provided by publisher.
Includes bibliographical references and index.
ISBN 978-0-7614-3006-3
1. New Jersey—Juvenile literature. I. Orr, Tamra. II. Title.
F134.3.M67 2009
974.9—dc22
2007038642

Editor: Christine Florie
Contributing Editor: Nikki Bruno Clapper
Publisher: Michelle Bisson
Art Director: Anahid Hamparian
Series Designer: Adam Mietlowski

Photo research by Connie Gardner

Cover photo by Gene Ahrens/SuperStock

The photographs in this book are used by permission and through the courtesy of: *SuperStock:* age
fotostock, back cover, 103; Purestock, 11; George Goodwin, 68; *Steve Greer Photography:* 8, 62, 66,
75, 80, 92, 96; *Gibson Stock Photography:* 100; *Alamy:* Phil Degginger, 12, 13; Jeff Greenberg, 51;
Tom Till, 88; Gail Mooney Kelly, 95; Realimage, 105(B); *Photo Researchers:* John Serrao, 14; Jeffrey
Lepore, 21; *Getty Images:* Ian Shive, 15; Panoramic Images, 22; Hulton Archive, 45; Stock Montage,
121; *Phil Degginger:* 17, 87; *Dembinsky Photo Associates:* John Pennoyer, 19; Phil Degginger, 76;
George E. Stewart, 105(T); *Digital RailRoad:* Phil Degginger, 23; Shawn Anderson, 117; *Corbis:*
Kenman Ward, 20; Bettmann: 26, 30, 35, 38, 41, 43, 123, 133; Corbis, 40; Reuters, 48, 64, 131;
James Leynse, 52; Noah K. Murray/Star Ledger, 53; Ed Murray/Star Ledger, 61; Kelly-Mooney
Photography, 65, 84, 97; Frank Conlon, 70; Ron Sachs, 71; Joseph Sohm, 89; Lee Snider, 91; Noah
K. Murray, 93; Bob Krist, 94; Picture Net, 101; James L. Amos, 102; Stephen Frink, 109; Ed Kashi,
113; Roger Ressmeyer, 119; Gilbert Iundt, 125; Petre Buzoianu, 127; Rebecca Cook, 129; *Associated
Press:* PR Newswire, 86; Charles Rex Arbogast, 137; *The Image Works:* Rhoda Sidney, 28; CP
Cushing/Classic Stock, 44; Nancy Richmond, 50; Monika Graff, 54; Jeff Greenberg, 58;
Topham, 79; *North Wind Picture Archives:* 32, 39.

Printed in Malaysia
3 5 6 4 2

# Contents

## New Jersey Is . . .

**New Jersey is a land of contrasts.**

"Diversity . . . that's the spirit of New Jersey."
—historian John T. Cunningham

**From its congested cities to its sprawling green farmland . . .**

"I was born in this town, this old brick city of sidewalks and gray steel winter shadows."
—poet Amiri Baraka describing Newark

"The Countrey is full of great and tall Oakes."
—explorer Robert Juet

**. . . from its ski slopes to its sandy beaches . . .**

"New Jersey is a playground for all seasons."
—former New Jersey governor Christine Todd Whitman

**. . . from its bustling turnpike to its serene Pinelands . . .**

"I thought New Jersey was just factories and smog. I was shocked to find beautiful flowering plants and trees like I've never seen before."
—visitor John Pifher

**. . . New Jersey beckons people to come and work, to come and play.**

"I am from New Jersey, where we are truly a unique bunch but we all have one thing in common: a sense of pride, hard work, and a deep loyalty to the state of New Jersey. No matter what part of Jersey you are from, it is a kinship that will last a lifetime."

—Nick, a native of Livingston

"[New Jersey is] my home. I think the way of saying it is, no matter where you go, you're always pulled back home."

—musician Jon Bon Jovi

"We have so much to be proud of in New Jersey . . . great people, beautiful shore, top notch universities and world class companies."

—Governor Jon Corzine

*New Jersey is a gem. Rich in beauty and rich in history, the Garden State has proven itself special through the years. This state is a place of extremes, including the largest seaport in the United States and the most diners. It draws people from all over the world to live and to visit. In fact, New Jersey is the most densely populated American state, averaging thirteen times more people per square mile than the national average. These people have brought with them their cultures, their talents, and their dreams. They have shaped the way of life in New Jersey just as they have shaped the soil, and they have made New Jersey the great state it is today.*

## Chapter One

# Hills, Valleys, and Beaches

There is an old saying that good things come in small packages. That saying is certainly true when it comes to New Jersey. Although it is the fifth-smallest state in the country, it is extraordinarily diverse. New Jersey offers everything from glacial lakes and wooded slopes to bustling cities and tidal marshes.

New Jersey's only true physical neighbor is New York State, with which it shares its 50-mile northern border. Three of New Jersey's borders consist of four different bodies of water—two rivers, a bay, and an ocean. The Hudson River and the Atlantic Ocean create New Jersey's eastern border. The Delaware River (with Pennsylvania on the other side) forms the western border and then spills into Delaware Bay, which creates the state's southern border. Even though New Jersey is small enough to drive across in about three hours, there is something for everyone in what space it has!

*New Jersey's Island Beach is one of the few remaining undeveloped beaches in the state. More than 10 miles of coastal dunes look almost exactly the same as they did when Henry Hudson first saw them four hundred years ago.*

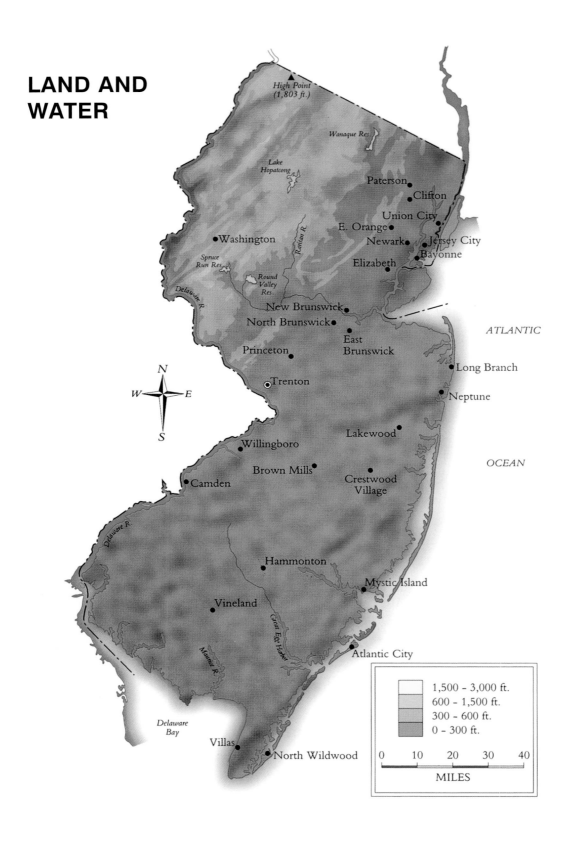

# LAND AND WATER

High Point
(1,803 ft.)

Wanaque Res.

Lake
Hopatcong

Paterson
Clifton
Union City
E. Orange
Newark
Jersey City
Bayonne
Elizabeth

Washington

Raritan R.

Spruce
Run Res.

Round
Valley
Res.

Delaware R.

New Brunswick
North Brunswick
East
Brunswick

Princeton

ATLANTIC

Long Branch

Trenton

Neptune

Lakewood

OCEAN

Willingboro

Brown Mills

Crestwood
Village

Camden

Delaware R.

Hammonton

Mystic Island

Vineland

Great Egg Harbor

Atlantic City

Maurice R.

Delaware
Bay

Villas

North Wildwood

N
W        E
S

| | |
|---|---|
| | 1,500 – 3,000 ft. |
| | 600 – 1,500 ft. |
| | 300 – 600 ft. |
| | 0 – 300 ft. |

0    10    20    30    40

MILES

The Appalachian Ridge and Valley Region of New Jersey lies in the northwestern corner of the state. Majestic red oaks—New Jersey's state tree—stand beside maples, birches, and elms. Flowering azaleas, rhododendrons, and purple violets—the state flower—provide color amid the greenery. This mountainous region includes the Kittatinny Mountains, where the Dutch mined copper in the mid-1600s.

The Delaware River, home to shad and trout, slices through the Kittatinny Mountains and forms the Delaware Water Gap, one of the most scenic areas in the eastern United States. The gap is a deep gorge that was formed millions of years ago as the Delaware River cut through the rock. Its steep walls rise more than 1,200 feet on each side. Some people enjoy hot air ballooning and plane gliding over this spectacular site.

At the base of the Kittatinny Mountains is the Appalachian Valley, where the soil is rich and dairy cattle graze on lush grass. A Dutch traveler in the 1600s called this area "the handsomest and pleasantest country that man can behold."

*The beautiful Delaware Water Gap National Recreation Area runs hundreds of miles to the Atlantic Ocean at Wilmington, Delaware.*

## THE FRANKLIN MINERALS

Franklin, New Jersey, is home to some unusual rocks. Millions of years ago, large pockets of zinc deep within the earth were altered in such a way that more than three hundred new minerals were formed. About thirty of these minerals have been found nowhere else on the planet.

Many of the Franklin minerals are fluorescent—they glow yellow, green, pink, lavender, and rose when placed under ultraviolet light. The Franklin Mineral Museum showcases these fantastic minerals and even gives rock hounds a chance to search for minerals outside.

The Highlands Region is southeast of the Appalachian Ridge and Valley Region. Here, lakes lie nestled among flat-topped ridges of hard rock. Thousands of years ago, a huge glacier carved the lakes into the rock. Hopatcong is the largest lake in New Jersey. Other large lakes in the highlands include Budd, Mohawk, Upper Greenwood, and Green Pond.

## THE PIEDMONT

Southeast of the highlands is the Piedmont, an area of gently rolling hills. Major rivers such as the Hudson, the Hackensack, the Raritan, and the Passaic flow through the Piedmont. These rivers powered the gristmills and textile mills of the booming industrial cities of Paterson, Newark, Elizabeth, and Jersey City. Slicing between two massive rocks in Paterson are the Great Falls of the Passaic River, a mighty gush of water spilling 70 feet down. Two Dutchmen who saw the falls in the 1600s described them as "a sight to be seen in order to observe the power and wonder of God."

Looming high above the Hudson River near Fort Lee is the Palisades, a 500-foot-tall, 13-mile-long cliff. In the early

*The Great Falls of the Passaic River is a 119-acre National Historic Landmark in Paterson.*

*The Palisades cliffs in Alpine provide lookout points where hikers can see beautiful views.*

1900s, silent movies were made in Fort Lee. One popular film series always showed the star in danger, often perched high on a cliff. That cliff was the Palisades. Scenes that left an audience in suspense eventually became known as cliff-hangers.

South of the Palisades are two great wetlands. Lying along the Hackensack River, the Meadowlands is a stretch of damp land that was left after a giant lake evaporated thousands of years ago. The area is rich in wildlife and vegetation, which manage to exist side by side with highways, office buildings, apartments, and a huge sports and entertainment complex called the Meadowlands. The Great Swamp, near Morristown, is also a former lake. People once suggested paving over this marshy, wooded area to make an airport, but citizens' groups convinced the government to protect the region, and the Great Swamp National Wildlife Refuge was created.

*This wooden trail through Basking Ridge's Great Swamp National Wildlife Refuge is part of its 7,600 acres of swamps, marshes, grassland, ponds, and ridges.*

About three-fifths of New Jersey is a gently rolling lowland called the Atlantic Coastal Plain. In the southwest, the Atlantic Coastal Plain contains fertile soil that is perfect for growing a variety of fruits and vegetables. This rich area gave New Jersey its official nickname, the Garden State. In this region, stately oak, maple, and pine trees create a safe haven for chipmunks, squirrels, and rabbits. Cardinals, blue jays, robins, and eastern goldfinches—the New Jersey state bird—build nests in the crooks of the branches.

The eastern part of the coastal plain is made up of pine forests, salt-water marshland, and sandy, gravelly soil. Deer, skunks, opossums, and raccoons live in the woodland, while wild ducks and geese prefer the marshland. At the far eastern edge of the Atlantic Coastal Plain lie New Jersey's 127 miles of white sandy beaches and dunes. The salty coastal waters abound with flounder, bluefish, crabs, oysters, and clams. Sand-pipers dance at the water's edge, while seagulls glide overhead. New Jersey forms a vital part of the Eastern Flyway, a major path for migra-tory birds on the East Coast.

One of the most intriguing features of the Atlantic Coastal Plain is the Pinelands, also called the Pine Barrens. The Pinelands is a vast area of forests, bogs, marshes, and swamps crisscrossed by streams and dot-ted with ponds. The water is tea-colored because organic material from cedar trees and iron seep out of the sandy soil. This soil is called Downer soil, and it is New Jersey's official state soil.

More than eight hundred plant species thrive in the sandy soil of the Pinelands. Plants provide food and shelter for more than three hundred species of mammals, birds, reptiles, and amphibians. Many of these plants and animals are unusual. They rely on the fragile environment for their existence. The rare curly-grass fern is a tiny plant that grows just above the waterline on the small mounds of earth where cedar trees grow in bogs. The curly-grass fern can survive only in this exact environment.

*As the sun sets over the water of the Pine Barrens, a flock of Canada geese flies in the last remaining light.*

## THE TRASH MUSEUM

Imagine falling into a landfill and being surrounded by nothing but used tires, old chicken wire, cardboard boxes, and aluminum cans. Visitors get a chance to experience this strange sensation when they visit the Trash Museum at the Meadowlands Environment Center and Museum in Lyndhurst. The Trash Museum conveys a clear and unforgettable message—recycle!

The center is built on an area of the Meadowlands where the Lenape Native Americans once dug clams and oysters. By the 1930s, people had turned the region into a dumping ground. In time, the garbage contaminated the soil and choked the wildlife and vegetation that once thrived there. Dangerous waste also seeped into nearby water and harmed the shellfish that once sustained the Lenape.

The turning point came in 1969, when the Hackensack Meadowlands Development Commission was formed. Commission leaders encouraged New Jerseyans to recycle their waste so that less of it would have to be dumped in landfills. Household dumping was eventually stopped in the Meadowlands. Remarkably, wildlife and vegetation have returned to the area. Even the water is clean again. The Meadowlands is proof that spoiled land can be revived and that recycling can help reduce waste.

The million-acre Pinelands region has towns and farms supporting more than 700,000 residents, but much of the area is protected by the government. Because of the unusual plants and animals that live there, the Pinelands was designated the country's first National Reserve in 1978 and an International Biosphere Reserve in 1983. In several state parks and forests, such as Double Trouble and Wharton, visitors hike or canoe through the quiet, mystical Pinelands. They can even swim in the strange, tea-colored water.

## NEW JERSEY WILDLIFE

Although New Jersey has a lot of people in it, the state still has room for diverse wildlife. White-tailed deer hide in the forests and turn up on suburban lawns. Black bears also live in New Jersey's forests, and they become controversial when they share space with humans. Striped skunks, eastern chipmunks, eastern gray squirrels, red and gray foxes, opossums, and raccoons are common mammals.

*A black bear and her cubs romp in the forest.*

New Jersey's shore birds include the herring gull, the sandpiper, and the green-backed heron. Further inland, the skies often contain chickadees, robins, cardinals, finches, and Baltimore orioles. The Indiana bat also once fluttered through darkening skies, but now it is considered endangered in the state.

New Jersey's waters are home to bass, trout, pike, and perch. Four species of turtles and three species of whales are threatened or endangered. The red salamander and northern kingfish are disappearing at a fast rate.

Thanks to New Jersey's coastal zones, fertile hills, and forested areas, many different kinds of plants and flowers can be found. Birch, beech,

*The green-backed heron catches its meals by dropping bait onto the water's surface and grabbing the fish that come to investigate.*

hickory, and elm trees grow here, as well as the red maple and twenty varieties of oak. Shrubs like the spicebush, staggerbush, and mountain laurel are common. Long stretches between trees are usually covered in pyxie, a small evergreen plant. Spring brings flowers of all sizes and colors, including butterfly weed, black-eyed Susans, and eastern dandelions. Two plant species, the bog asphodel and the Knieskern's beaked-rush, are found only in New Jersey. The state contains 70 percent of the world's population of swamp pink, an endangered, bright pink flower cluster that blooms in the early spring. The biggest clumps of this flower are found in Cumberland County.

*Swamp pink pops up from the ground in late March. By summer it is in full bloom.*

## THE PINE BARRENS TREE FROG

The Pine Barrens tree frog, one of New Jersey's endangered species, is a tiny creature, just over 1.5 inches long. Its call is a distinct series of honks that sound like "quonk, quonk, quonk." It is emerald green with a white and purple band that runs along its sides from head to toe. The undersides of its hind legs are yellowish orange.

The Pine Barrens tree frog depends on the swampy soil and acidic water of the Pinelands. Although this species also exists in some Southern states, it does not live anywhere in New Jersey except in the Pinelands. If the amount of acid in the water or the level of the water in the Pinelands were to change, the Pine Barrens tree frog would not be able to survive there. Its habitat is carefully protected, however. By limiting the development that can take place in the Pinelands, New Jersey officials are trying to ensure that the Pine Barrens tree frog and other creatures can continue to thrive in an unspoiled region.

"I love the change of seasons," said Victoria Browning of Cherry Hill. "I enjoy the lovely spring flowers, especially the tulips, and the mix of colors of the autumn leaves. I always look forward to going to the shore in the summer, and I really don't mind the winter. Everything is so quiet and peaceful during a snowfall."

Many New Jerseyans believe they have the best of everything when it comes to weather. Although summers tend to be humid, the shore and the mountains offer relief. The shore's cool breezes and refreshing ocean waves provide comfort. Rain keeps the inland areas green throughout the summer, especially in the northern part of the state. Then, beginning in late September, the lush green gives way to brilliant autumn colors as the leaves turn shades of red, orange, and yellow. The air becomes crisp during the fall and hints at the chilly winter months ahead.

The average January temperature in New Jersey is 31 degrees Fahrenheit. The average July temperature is 75 °F. The northern part of the state receives more snowfall than the southern part.

*The edge of the Lamington River is decorated vividly with the vibrant gold, orange, red, and brown shades of autumn.*

Over the years, New Jersey has fallen victim to hurricanes, nor'easters, blizzards, ice storms, and even an occasional tornado. The relentless wind and rain of hurricanes and nor'easters flatten trees and damage buildings as they pound, sometimes for days. Along the coast, surging tides and waves wash away beaches, boardwalks, and houses. Blizzards and ice storms snap electrical wires and cripple traffic. "Bad storms don't come through very often, but when they do, they're real beauties," said Hank Susen, a senior citizen who has lived in New Jersey all his life.

## PROTECTING THE ENVIRONMENT

New Jersey is the nation's most densely populated state, and pollutants from cars, development, and industry threaten its environment. State officials strive to control air pollution and to protect the state's water supply. Rainwater that falls on roads picks up accumulated oil and gasoline from cars and trucks. The water then carries these pollutants into nearby waterways. Chemicals and fertilizers used on lawns also run off into waterways during rains. New Jerseyans have been asked to help in simple ways, such as planting grass and trees and avoiding the use of lawn chemicals and fertilizers. New grass and trees help rainwater soak into the ground so that fewer pollutants wash into waterways.

New Jersey's heavy boat traffic also threatens the state's waters. Government officials are working with marine associations to reduce the amount of sewage that boats release into the water. Many uncaring people have dumped their boats' waste tanks into New Jersey's ocean, bays, and rivers. To encourage people not to do this, workers have set up special stations where boaters can pump out their waste tanks.

These efforts have already paid off. The number of ocean fish, such as striped bass, Atlantic mackerel, and Atlantic herring, has increased since 2001. Even dolphins appear in offshore waters now. New Jersey's clammers have something to rejoice about, too. "For the first time in twenty-five years, we opened more than 600 acres for seasonal unrestricted clamming in the Navesink River," said former governor Christine Todd Whitman. Still, New Jerseyans will have to keep working hard to ensure that the state's waters are clean and safe for people and wildlife alike.

The environment continues to be a high priority for the people of New Jersey. In 2005, the New Jersey Conservation Foundation helped preserve over 2,800 acres of land, including forests, farmland, and natural resources. In partnership with other public agencies, the group formed the largest wetlands restoration program in the northeastern United States. In late 2007, New Jersey voted yes on the Green Acres, Farmland, Blue Acres, and Historic Preservation Bond Act of 2007. This entitles the state to $200 million in funds to keep New Jersey's open space, farmland, and historic preservation programs going for one more year, as well as to help with flood control.

## Chapter Two

# Mighty New Jersey

Ten thousand years before the first Europeans explored the New Jersey area, it was home to thousands of Native Americans. By the time the white explorers and settlers arrived, the native peoples they encountered called themselves the Lenape, a name that means "original people." Explorers often referred to the Lenape as the Delaware, a name that the tribe still carries today.

## THE LENAPE

The Lenape relied on hunting for their survival. Deer, foxes, squirrels, minks, raccoons, and even bears provided them with nutritious meat and warm furs. The Lenape also hunted wild geese and turkeys. The birds' leftover feathers adorned men's heads. Deerskins served as clothing for both men and women. The Lenape supplemented their diet by planting vegetables. Beans, squash, and corn grew well in the rich soil. The Lenape also enjoyed the abundant blueberries, strawberries, and cranberries that grew wild on the land.

*Throughout most of its history, New Jersey has been known for its successful industries. Here, a woman works at a munitions factory during World War I.*

Each spring, the Lenape left the region's forested interior and journeyed by foot to the seashore, where they spent several months. Footstep upon footstep, they packed the earth beneath their feet and created permanent paths through the woods and over land. White settlers—and today's New Jerseyans—later used these trails as roads. Along the coast, the Lenape took advantage of the plentiful fish and shellfish. They ate some of the seafood fresh during the summer and smoke-dried the rest for winter use in the villages.

The Lenape lived in round wigwams or rectangular longhouses. These structures were constructed from young trees, called saplings, set in the ground with other saplings tied to them. This framework was then covered with bark, offering shelter and shade. Villages often included a rectangular council house, along with a sweat house for the men to use. Some of the villages were surrounded with log walls for protection. Traveling in canoes crafted from logs, the Lenape used rivers and streams as their highways.

*This Lenape village was re-created in Waterloo Village.*

They shaped their canoes by burning parts of logs and then scooping out the charred wood.

While Lenape men hunted, women did most of the child care. Women frequently carried their babies on their backs by attaching them securely to long, straight cradleboards. This kept the baby close and safe, yet freed women's arms so that they could do their work. Both men and women spent time developing crafts such as storytelling, basket weaving, and music, as well as traditional medicine.

Lenape women typically wore knee-length skirts, while men wore a type of pants known as breechcloths and leggings. People wore deerskin moccasins on their feet, and some wore beaded headbands. Both men and women painted their faces with various colors and patterns to honor special days. While women kept their hair in long braids, men either wore Mohawks or shaved their heads except for a scalp lock—one long streak of hair on the top of their heads.

## THE EXPLORERS

When Giovanni de Verrazano of Italy crossed the Atlantic Ocean from France in 1524, he became the first European to explore what would become New Jersey. His visit was short and had little impact on the land or the people who lived there. Nearly one hundred years would pass before the Lenape would face change.

In 1609, Henry Hudson, an Englishman employed by the Dutch, sailed across the Atlantic. His mission was to find a waterway that would pass through North America and lead to Asia, where gold, jewels, and other riches awaited. Hudson never found the passage, however. Instead, he went ashore in what would become New Jersey and traded with the Lenape. Hudson's visit opened the door for traders and settlers to come to the new land.

*In this painting, called* Hudson, the Dreamer, *explorer Henry Hudson is shown talking with Native Americans in 1609.*

## THE SETTLERS

The Dutch and Swedish settlers who arrived in the 1630s were the first white people to inhabit New Jersey. For the first time, the Lenape had to share their land. Early on, the relationship between the Native Americans and the Europeans was friendly. The welcoming ways of the Lenape enabled the settlers to establish themselves. The Native Americans taught the settlers about hunting, fishing, trapping, and growing plants. They gave the Europeans land in exchange for clothing, guns, knives, and trinkets such as glass beads. The Lenape also traded animal furs with the settlers. The furs were taken to Europe, where they were sold to coat and hat manufacturers.

The fur trade was so profitable that conflict arose between the Dutch and the Swedes. By 1655, the Dutch had forced all but a few Swedes out of the area, and in 1660, they set up New Jersey's first permanent European village, which they named Bergen. Over time, Bergen—now called Jersey City—grew and prospered. Meanwhile, tension mounted between the Dutch and the Lenape. Their quarrels over taxation, land, trade, and lifestyle resulted in bloodshed on both sides.

## ENGLAND RULES

In 1664, England took control of the land that the Dutch had settled. Two Englishmen, Lord John Berkeley and Sir George Carteret, were given a portion of the land. Carteret had served as governor of Jersey, an island in the English Channel, and the land was named New Jersey in his honor.

Berkeley and Carteret wanted to treat the land as a business enterprise. They hoped that rental fees and trade would bring them money. This would only be possible if settlers agreed to live there, however. To encourage people to make this wilderness their home, Berkeley and Carteret promised them low rent as well as religious and political freedom. Their offer was so appealing that many settlers journeyed from colonies farther north to make New Jersey their home.

In 1675, Berkeley sold his share of New Jersey to Edward Byllynge and John Fenwick, who were members of a religious group called the Quakers. The colony was divided into two sections, West Jersey and East Jersey. The Quakers settled in West Jersey, which became the first Quaker colony in America. Six years later, William Penn, also a Quaker, and his associates bought East Jersey. People began to journey across the Atlantic from England, Scotland, and Ireland to take advantage of what New Jersey had to offer.

*This Quaker meetinghouse in Burlington was built in 1683 but was torn down and replaced in 1785. It is still used today for meetings and conferences.*

## A SETTLER'S LIFE

Farming was the New Jersey settlers' most important activity. To feed their families, they grew grains, fruits, and vegetables and raised livestock. Some settlers were also involved in businesses. Tanneries turned cowhides into leather products, sawmills turned trees into lumber, and gristmills turned wheat into flour.

As the 1600s came to a close, people began to argue about who owned the land. The settlers resented paying rent. This tension finally led to rioting, and by 1702, the people who supposedly owned East and West Jersey gave up ownership. England then united the two colonies.

During the 1700s, farming expanded as the colonists began selling their crops in the nearby cities of New York and Philadelphia. Iron mining became profitable as well. Iron ore was plentiful in the hills of northern New Jersey. In southern New Jersey, bog iron, a low-grade form of iron that collects along riverbanks, was common. Throughout the colony, vast forests supplied the charcoal that fueled iron furnaces. Many men made their living by chopping down trees. The abundance of trees also prompted settlers to set up sawmills, where the wood was cut into lumber and shipped overseas or to nearby cities. In 1739, Caspar Wistar opened a glassmaking factory in Salem. The Wistarberg Works turned out bottles, jars, and windowpanes for the colonies.

Fishing and whaling were also profitable industries. Boats with five or six crewmen left from Long Beach Island and Cape May to harpoon whales. Whale carcasses were towed onto the beach, where they were cut up immediately. The flesh was cooked in huge iron kettles, and the oil was sold throughout the colonies for use in oil lamps and for making candles and soap.

## GROWTH MEANS CHANGE

As New Jersey grew, the Lenape faced dramatic change. European-borne diseases, such as measles and smallpox, had killed many of them. The survivors found themselves at odds with the settlers over how the land should be used. Because the Lenape relied on hunting for their survival, preserving the forests meant everything to them.

On the other hand, the colonists depended on farming and on their iron, lumber, and glass industries. They wanted to clear the forests to fuel their furnaces and to create farmland.

Most Lenape left New Jersey for New York and Pennsylvania in search of a better life. In 1758, the few hundred Lenape who had stayed in New Jersey were offered a 3,044-acre tract of land in Burlington County where they could live undisturbed. The Lenape lived on this reservation, called Brotherton, until 1802, when most left New Jersey to join the others who had gone before them.

## THE REVOLUTIONARY WAR

During the 1760s, unrest began to simmer in the colonies because of a series of laws passed by the British parliament. These laws restricted colonial trade and set high taxes on items such as tea. By 1774, tension was so high that a group of angry New Jerseyans dressed as Native Americans and burned a shipload of British tea in Greenwich. This event became known as the Greenwich Tea Burning. It was similar to the Boston Tea Party, which had taken place a year earlier in Massachusetts.

Although some colonists felt that they should stay loyal to Britain in spite of the strict new laws, many believed that becoming independent of Britain was the only way to go. They put their intentions in writing when they signed the Declaration of Independence in July 1776.

General George Washington led the Continental army throughout the Revolutionary War. Much of the army's ammunition was made in New Jersey's ironworks, and the food for his soldiers came from New Jersey farms.

Washington and his troops met with disappointment early in the war, but then Washington came up with a plan. He knew that the Hessians—Germans fighting on England's side—would celebrate Christmas in the

Barracks, a large building in Trenton. Figuring that the Hessians would fall into a deep sleep after the night's festivities, Washington planned a surprise attack. Late on Christmas night, 1776, Washington and 2,400 of his troops crossed the icy Delaware River in a snowstorm and walked 8 miles to the Barracks. On the morning of December 26, Washington's army bombarded the unsuspecting Hessians and succeeded in taking nearly one thousand prisoners. The spot in Titusville where Washington and his men came ashore is now called Washington Crossing State Park. Every Christmas, people reenact the crossing of the Delaware at the park.

*An important moment in history is captured in Emanuel Gottlieb Leutze's painting,* Washington Crossing the Delaware, *created in 1851.*

# THE BATTLE OF TRENTON

Late on Christmas night, 1776, George Washington's ragged army rowed across the icy Delaware River and fell upon a 1,200-man Hessian force in Trenton as the men slept off their Christmas celebration. This event happened after a long series of military setbacks for Washington and the Continental army. "The Battle of Trenton" commemorates the much-needed victory.

Our object was the Hessian band,
That dared invade fair freedom's land,
        And quarter in that place.
Great Washington he led us on,
Whose streaming flag in storm or sun
        Had never known disgrace.

In silent march we passed the night,
Each soldier panting for the fight,
        Though quite benumbed with frost.
Greene, on the left, at six began.
The right was led by Sullivan,
        Who ne'er a moment lost.

Their pickets stormed, the alarm was spread,
That rebels risen from the dead
        Were marching into town.
Some scampered here, some scampered there,
And some for action did prepare;
        But soon their arms lay down.

Twelve hundred servile miscreants,
With all their colors, guns and tents,
        Were trophies of the day.
The frolic o'er, the bright canteen
In center, front and rear was seen,
        Driving fatigue away.

Now, brothers of the patriot bands,
Let's sing deliverance from the hands
        Of arbitrary sway.
And as our life is but a span,
Let's touch the tankard while we can,
        In memory of that day.

The Battle of Monmouth was fought in New Jersey on the scorching summer day of June 28, 1778. Legend has it that Molly Pitcher, the wife of a soldier, dipped water from a nearby well to soothe the men's parched mouths throughout the battle. During the Revolutionary War, soldiers' wives were allowed to travel with their husbands, so it was not unusual for Molly to be on the battlefield. What was unusual, however, was that later in the battle, Molly manned one of the cannons. Today, at the Monmouth Battlefield State Park near Freehold, visitors can see the Molly Pitcher Well.

*Molly Pitcher shows her bravery at the Battle of Monmouth.*

Washington and his troops finally achieved victory in 1783. On December 18, 1787, New Jersey signed the U.S. Constitution and became the third state in the Union. Trenton became the state capital in 1790, and it remains the capital today.

### BECOMING AN INDUSTRIAL LEADER

In 1791, Alexander Hamilton, secretary of the U.S. treasury, chose the land around the Great Falls of the Passaic as the site for a factory town. According to his plans, the water of the falls would supply power to run factories, which would manufacture cotton cloth. His plan worked, and Paterson became the first planned industrialized city in the United States.

In 1825, John Stevens built the nation's first steam locomotive in Hoboken. Two years later, Thomas Rogers began building steam locomotives in Paterson, which became the hub of locomotive production.

*Johnny Bull was the first locomotive to run on the Camden & Amboy Railroad, the state's first official railroad.*

By the end of the century, thousands of steam locomotives had been manufactured there. In 1840, silk manufacturing also took hold, and Paterson became known as Silk City.

Meanwhile, other New Jersey cities were buzzing with activity. Trenton was manufacturing iron, textiles, and pottery. Newark was turning out a vast array of goods, including leather products and jewelry. Jersey City workers were making soap, bricks, and steel. Glassworks were busy in the southern part of the state.

*In the late nineteenth and early twentieth centuries, silk factory employees worked long hours in the city of Paterson.*

New Jersey's industries prospered because of improvements in transportation. Canals and railroads built in the 1830s connected New Jersey's cities to New York and Philadelphia. People immigrated from Ireland and Germany to build the canals and railroads and to work in the flourishing factories.

## THE CIVIL WAR

From the time Europeans first settled the East Coast, they had taken Africans there to work as slaves. Many Northerners, including the Quakers, were against slavery, and they helped slaves gain freedom. In 1804, New Jersey passed a law to free its slaves gradually. In the Southern states, however, slavery continued.

When Abraham Lincoln, who opposed slavery, was elected president of the United States in 1860, some Southerners saw their way of life slipping away. They decided to break away from the United States and form the Confederate States of America. Northerners did not want the Southern states to separate from the Union. The result was the Civil War. Although no battles were fought on its soil, New Jersey sent 88,000 men into the Union army.

The North's thriving industries and booming population eventually made the difference in the war. The factories and farms of New Jersey and other Northern states supplied the Union army.

*New Jersey fought on the Union's side in the Civil War. Pictured here are Union soldiers.*

The Confederate army did not have the same resources. In the end, the lack of food and supplies doomed the Confederate army, which surrendered in 1865. The war was finally over, and so was slavery.

New Jersey prospered after the war. In 1869, a dentist named Thomas Bramwell Welch, based in Vineland, found a way to make juice from local grapes. This was the beginning of the Welch's Grape Juice Company. The year proved just as prosperous for Joseph Campbell in Camden. Taking advantage of New Jersey's plentiful peas and tomatoes, he opened a canning plant, and the Campbell Soup Company was born.

In the 1870s, life-changing innovations were being developed in Menlo Park, where Thomas Edison invented the phonograph and perfected the electric light. In Paterson, John Philip Holland built a 14-foot submarine that he took to the bottom of the Passaic River in 1878. His efforts led to the development of today's submarines.

During the final decades of the nineteenth century, the Johnson & Johnson medical supply company established itself in New Brunswick and began manufacturing gauze and adhesive tape. Eldridge R. Johnson built talking machines that played flat disks, or records, instead of the cylinders used for Edison's phonograph. Johnson's Victor Talking Machine Company in Camden soon became the world's largest producer of phonograph records.

One of the era's greatest breakthroughs was the development of motion pictures in 1892 by Thomas Edison, who had moved his laboratory to West Orange. By the early 1900s, motion pictures had become so popular that a busy filmmaking industry cropped up in Fort Lee.

*In April 1898, Irish inventor John Philip Holland pops his head out of one of his own submarines, the* Holland VI.

## FORT LEE, THE MOVIE CAPITAL

Believe it or not, Fort Lee, New Jersey, was once the movie capital of America, and Hollywood, California, was just an ordinary town. Thanks to the moving pictures developed by Thomas Edison, the filmmaking industry took off in Fort Lee in the early 1900s.

New Jersey's cities, beaches, mountains, and farms were the back-drops for movie after movie. A section of Fort Lee looked exactly like an Old West town, so even filming Westerns was a cinch. Big-name stars such as Mary Pickford, Douglas Fairbanks, Lillian Gish, and Lionel and Ethel Barrymore walked Fort Lee's streets.

Fort Lee's heyday did not last, however. When a top filmmaker named D. W. Griffith journeyed to California and made a film in Hollywood, a shadow was cast over Fort Lee. The sunny, mild weather of California proved irresistible, and the other filmmakers also headed west. By 1925, New Jersey's film industry was gone.

As the nineteenth century melded into the twentieth, New Jersey's industries kept on rolling. In the cities, the manufacture of oil, steel, rubber, chemicals, electrical goods, and apparel bolstered the economy. In rural areas, canneries and glass factories kept going strong. Dairy and poultry businesses also took hold, and residents of nearby cities welcomed shipments of farm-fresh milk, eggs, and poultry.

With the growth of New Jersey's farm production and industries came the need for more workers. Between the late 1800s and early 1900s, hundreds of thousands of people came from Germany, Italy, Ireland, Poland, and Russia to work in New Jersey. So many immigrants flooded into the state that by 1910, more than half of New Jersey's residents were foreign-born or had foreign-born parents.

## WARS AND DEPRESSION

The United States entered World War I in 1917. During the war, New Jersey's huge shipyards turned out battleships. Its factories manufactured ammunition, chemicals, and fabric for uniforms and blankets.

About a decade after the war ended, the United States found itself in the Great Depression. People all over the country lost their jobs, and banks failed. Even New Jersey was hit hard. Many of the state's factories closed, and some workers were forced to stand in long breadlines for food. People had to go without many everyday items. "I can remember my mother cutting pieces of cardboard

*In January 1916, American troops leave Camp Merritt for France to fight in World War I.*

to put in the bottom of my shoes," said a senior citizen who grew up in Camden. "We had a pair of everyday shoes and a pair of dress shoes, and when the soles wore out, that was it. We had to make do with the cardboard. Otherwise, we just had socks on the bottoms of our feet."

The nation's economy picked up when the United States entered World War II in 1941. New Jersey again produced ammunition, chemicals, tanks, and battleships, as well as communications equipment. Paterson became the nation's leading airplane-engine manufacturing center. New Jersey also supported the war effort with its people. More than 500,000 New Jersey residents served in the armed forces during World War II.

## NEW JERSEY TODAY

After World War II, New Jersey's economy was strong. The chemicals, medicines, electronics, and foods that the state produced were selling well. Its research firms were developing technology that would change the way people lived. Solar cells, lasers, transistors, and satellite communications were developed at Bell Laboratories in Murray Hill.

The state's densely populated cities began to spill into rural areas. Housing developments were built on farmland outside the cities, and many families who could afford to move left the overcrowded cities. Suburbs around Philadelphia and New York City were especially popular because residents could commute to jobs in these cities.

While New Jersey's suburbs blossomed, its cities wilted. As people and industries moved away, buildings and public services were abandoned. In time, the cities' African-American residents rebelled against discrimination and the neglect of their neighborhoods. In July 1967, riots broke out in several cities around the state. The worst was in Newark, where twenty-six people were killed and more than a thousand were injured.

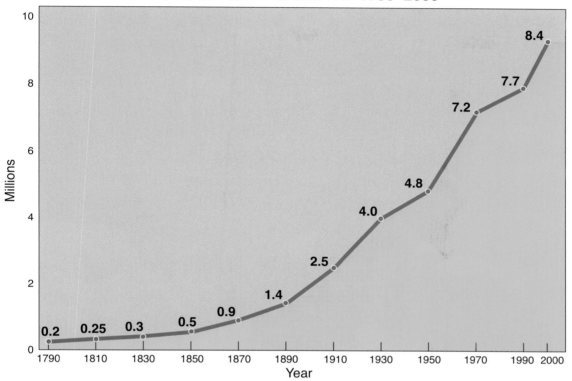

**POPULATION GROWTH: 1790–2000**

Millions

Year

0.2  0.25  0.3  0.5  0.9  1.4  2.5  4.0  4.8  7.2  7.7  8.4

Not until the 1980s was an effort made to brighten New Jersey's cities. Urban renewal projects attracted businesses and called for improvements to the state's most run-down cities. Much work remains to be done, but growth continues to occur.

New Jersey is a state whose people are not afraid to tackle controversial issues. In 1982, the legislature reinstated the death penalty for certain types of murder. Five years later, the male-only eating clubs at Princeton University were ordered to admit women. In 1997, New Jersey became the first state to remove regulations preventing same-sex couples from adopting children.

*During Hurricane Floyd in September 1999, many residents had to be moved by state police boat after the Raritan River's banks flooded most of Bound Brook.*

As of 2007, New Jersey recognizes civil unions of same-sex couples. In 2005, New Jersey was the first state to award public funding for stem cell research.

New Jersey has weathered some tough challenges in recent years. In 1999, Hurricane Floyd caused major flood damage throughout the region when almost 12 inches of rain fell throughout the state. On September 11, 2001, almost seven hundred New Jerseyans were killed during the terrorist attack on New York's World Trade Center and the Pentagon in Washington, D.C. As New Jersey moves into the twenty-first century, it continues to draw on the strengths of its land and people, as it has for hundreds of years. "New Jersey may be small, but it's mighty," said a proud New Jerseyan. "There isn't a day that goes by that I don't feel lucky to live here."

## Chapter Three
# A Melting Pot

The residents of New Jersey have roots all over the world. A large majority of New Jerseyans are the descendants of Europeans who came to farm the land, to build canals and railroads, and to work in factories.

African Americans account for about 15 percent of New Jersey's population. The state's first black residents were Africans who were brought to the colony as slaves. Later, blacks migrated to New Jersey from the Southern states to work in factories. Today, many blacks are coming from Caribbean nations such as Jamaica and Haiti. Until recently, African Americans were the largest ethnic minority in the state.

The Latino, or Hispanic, population is now equal to that of African Americans. The number of Latinos moving to New Jersey from Puerto Rico, Cuba, and Central and South America has been rising quickly over the last few years.

*African Americans make up one of New Jersey's largest cultural groups.*

*New Jersey's population becomes more diverse every year. These teens are hanging out after school.*

*A Puerto Rican migrant worker stops to sample a ripe tomato from the harvest in Swedesboro.*

The greatest growth has been in the Puerto Rican community, which primarily lives in the cities of Newark, Jersey City, Elizabeth, Paterson, and Passaic.

A smaller but significant percentage of New Jersey's residents are Asians, who come primarily from Vietnam, Japan, China, Korea, the Philippines, and India. Between 1990 and 2000, the number of New Jersey residents from India tripled. New Jersey has the fifth-largest Asian population in the country.

New Jersey's small Native-American population includes Eskimos and Aleuts. Many of them are descendants of Lenape and Tuscadora Native Americans who married Dutch settlers, African-American slaves, and British and German soldiers.

Old Bridge is home to a strong Indian community. Here, a group of dancers from the Sudhamini Dance Academy performs a traditional dance.

New Jersey's suburbs are home to millions of people who commute into the cities to work. For every person who commutes, however, there are many who do not. Lots of big-city companies have moved their offices to the suburbs, and thousands of small local businesses employ suburban residents. Housing developments, shopping malls, and traffic congestion are common in New Jersey's suburbs, and life tends to be hurried and hectic. "I do my grocery shopping late at night to avoid the crowds," said a woman who lives in a suburb of New York City. "I can't stand to fight for a parking place and then go in the store and wait in line."

*On August 14, 2003, a major power outage shut down trains and subways and caused traffic nightmares throughout the East Coast. Here, commuters from New York City to New Jersey line up for a bus near the Lincoln Tunnel.*

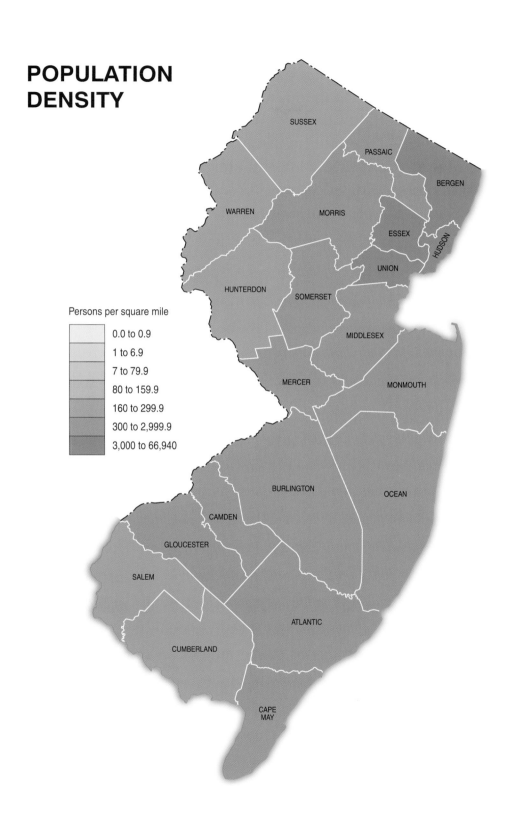

# POPULATION DENSITY

Persons per square mile

- 0.0 to 0.9
- 1 to 6.9
- 7 to 79.9
- 80 to 159.9
- 160 to 299.9
- 300 to 2,999.9
- 3,000 to 66,940

SUSSEX

PASSAIC

BERGEN

WARREN

MORRIS

ESSEX

HUDSON

UNION

HUNTERDON

SOMERSET

MIDDLESEX

MERCER

MONMOUTH

BURLINGTON

OCEAN

CAMDEN

GLOUCESTER

SALEM

ATLANTIC

CUMBERLAND

CAPE MAY

The farther reaches of the state are less populated, and residents seem more laid-back. The state's once-quiet coastal areas have seen amazing growth since the mid-1980s, however. Many young families and senior citizens have left cities in the northern part of the state to live at the seashore year-round. They take advantage of lower housing prices, property taxes, and crime rates. "We used to live in Paterson," said eleven-year-old John Ellio of Brick. "We lived in a duplex and we hardly had any yard at all. Here we have our own house and a nice yard. The best part is that my dad bought a boat for fishing. I love to fish!"

Most of the Pinelands is still rural. Towns are tiny, and traffic jams are unheard-of. Residents pride themselves on keeping life simple and unhurried. Over the years, the people who live in the quietest areas have become known as Pineys. Years ago, some Pineys made a living by gathering ferns, moss, and leaves of plants that grow in the Pinelands and selling them to flower shops to be used in floral arrangements. Others cut down cedar trees and sold the wood to boatbuilders. Yet others farmed blueberries—first developed commercially in New Jersey—and cranberries. Today, the children and grandchildren of the old-time Pineys continue to rely on the land. "My family has lived here for generations," said a cranberry farmer, "and we wouldn't live anywhere else. This land has been good to us. This is our home."

## BIG CITIES

New Jersey's cities wrestle with the problems common in cities across the United States. Many of the factories and other businesses that once thrived in the cities have shut down, moved to the suburbs, or moved out of the state. With this change came a dramatic loss of jobs for inner-city residents and, in turn, a dark cloud of poverty.

## THE JERSEY DEVIL: A PINELANDS LEGEND

Deep in the Pinelands on a stormy night in 1735, a woman struggled to give birth to her thirteenth child. Candlelight flickered against the bare walls indoors, while lightning darted through the black sky outdoors. With a final groan from the woman, a healthy baby boy emerged. Within seconds, his delicate human features gave way to gruesome monstrous features. The beast had the body of a kangaroo, the head of a dog, the face of a horse, the feet of a pig, the tail of a serpent, and the wings of a bat. It shot smoke from its nostrils, bellowed an eerie cry, and disappeared up the chimney and out into the darkness. So began the legend of the Jersey Devil.

Over the years, people have blamed droughts, crop failures, and fish diseases on the Jersey Devil. In January 1909, it supposedly spent a week terrorizing people from Camden to Trenton. Hundreds of people reported seeing the demon riding on wagons, killing animals, and breaking into homes. Afterward, it disappeared into the forest. In 1966, more than twenty ducks, geese, cats, and dogs were killed mysteriously on a farm in the heart of the Pinelands. Was it the work of the Jersey Devil? Just ask a New Jerseyan!

The flight out of cities also led to an epidemic of abandoned buildings. Over time, some of these crumbling buildings became drug houses, where people gather to buy and to use drugs. Where there are drugs, there are often guns. Some inner-city children live in constant fear of being caught in gun crossfire. "My mamma tells us to get down on the floor and crawl under a bed when we hear gunfire," said a seven-year-old Newark girl.

Violence isn't the only problem. One Camden teenager said, "Our streets aren't just spoiled by violence, they're spoiled by pollution and garbage, too." In Camden and other cities, state funding is helping to correct some of these problems. Old, unsafe buildings have been knocked down, and new ones have been built in their place. Some improvements are as simple as

*Student volunteers paint over graffiti on a building in Newark.*

putting up street signs and making sure garbage is collected. A cleaner, brighter appearance can help cities attract new businesses, which will boost the economy and provide jobs. In Camden, former mayor Milton Milan said, "Camden is open for business!"

## CELEBRATING DIVERSITY

New Jersey's cities are suffering, but they are filled with treasures—including their people. Some of the state's best performing-arts theaters, museums, and art galleries are found there. New Jersey's cities are also bubbling with ethnic culture. Many city restaurants, especially in the northern and central regions of the state, cater to the tastes of customers from around the world. Restaurants in Newark please the city's large Portuguese-American population by serving traditional Portuguese dishes.

"My favorite dish is rabbit with rice, and you don't find that in just any restaurant," said Antonio Penedo, a native of Portugal. Trenton boasts an Italian district, where restaurants serve classic Italian and Italian-American dishes.

## NO-COOK CRANBERRY RELISH

New Jersey is one of the nation's leading cranberry-producing states. At the state's cranberry festivals, visitors tour the cranberry bogs, eat cranberry muffins and cranberry sherbet, and drink cranberry juice. Cranberry jelly and relish are sold to take home and enjoy later. Have an adult help you make your own cranberry relish.

1 pound fresh cranberries (chopped coarsely—a food processor works well)
1 apple (chopped, with peel)
1 fresh orange (chopped, without peel)
1 small can of crushed pineapple
1/2 cup walnuts (chopped)
3/4 cup granulated sugar
one 3-ounce package of strawberry or cherry gelatin

In a large bowl, dissolve the gelatin in one cup of hot water. Mix the remaining ingredients into the gelatin and stir well. Refrigerate, and then enjoy!

# ETHNIC NEW JERSEY

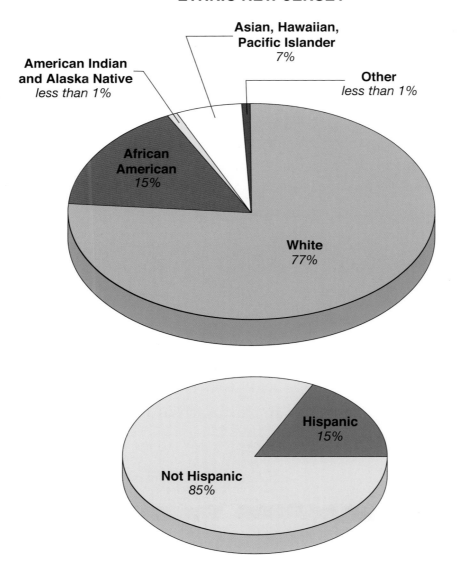

Asian, Hawaiian, Pacific Islander
7%

American Indian and Alaska Native
less than 1%

Other
less than 1%

African American
15%

White
77%

Hispanic
15%

Not Hispanic
85%

Note: A person of Cuban, Mexican, Puerto Rican, South or Central American, or other Spanish culture or origin, regardless of race, is defined as Hispanic.

Residents of Irish and German descent enjoy annual festivities that celebrate their heritage. Traditional Irish music and green costumes are highlights of the St. Patrick's Day parade in Seaside Heights. Yodelers and German foods, such as sauerbraten and Wiener schnitzel, can be found at Oktoberfest in Stanhope and Egg Harbor City.

Many immigrants from the Caribbean, particularly Haiti, have chosen East and West Orange as their new homes. Foods made from guava and papaya sell well, and hot Haitian bread is a favorite. Many residents of Perth Amboy come from Central and South America. More than half the city's population speaks Spanish at home.

Edgewater's large Asian population is reflected in the Yaohan U.S.A. Corp., a unique Asian shopping center. The center's stores and

*Girls in full costume celebrate Asian-American Heritage Month in Bridgewater.*

restaurants offer Japanese, Chinese, and Korean products and foods. In Edison, Woodbridge, and Iselin, it is not unusual to see Indian-American women dressed in saris, the native dresses of India. These long, flowing dresses are made of beautiful, brightly colored fabric.

About 1,500 families of Nanticoke Lenape still live in southern New Jersey. The state government has recognized their tribal council since 1978. The Nanticoke Lenape form the largest active tribe of Native Americans in New Jersey. Lenape culture is celebrated in Belvidere at the Return to Beaver Creek Powwow. Dancers in beaded costumes and jewelry perform to the beat of Native-American music, while talented artists display elaborate creations.

*New Jersey's Nanticoke Lenni-Lenape community holds a powwow each year.*

## MANY PEOPLE, LITTLE LAND

In recent years New Jerseyans have faced a worsening case of urban sprawl. Urban sprawl happens when a metropolitan area grows outward quickly and ends up hurting the environment, increasing traffic and air pollution, crowding the schools, and even driving up taxes.

For many years, New Jerseyans have moved out of the cities and into the suburbs. This movement of people puts a strain on resources. More roads have to be built, more businesses are needed to serve the area, and more public utilities have to be provided. In the meantime, more traffic fills the roads. The cycle is endless, and the price is usually the health of the environment.

State officials are working hard to find solutions to the problem of urban sprawl. Suggested remedies include improving and expanding mass-transportation systems and supporting the open-space laws that exist in some areas. Under these laws, communities agree to buy open lots within their neighborhoods and to leave them undeveloped or make them into parks or playgrounds.

## A RELIGIOUS MIX

The ethnic mix of New Jersey's residents translates into a diverse group of religions. Catholics, Protestants, Jews, Hindus, Muslims, Buddhists, and people of other faiths live side by side in New Jersey. During the 1600s, the Dutch set up the Reformed Church, and the English established Puritan and Quaker settlements. Presbyterians, Lutherans, and Methodists arrived in the 1700s. In 1848, Jews established New Jersey's first synagogue in Newark.

The first Roman Catholic parish was established in 1814. In the 1800s, so many Catholics emigrated from Ireland and Italy that the number of Catholics in New Jersey soared. Today, Catholics are the state's largest religious group.

In New Jersey's many Indian communities, the celebration of Deepavali is an important tradition. Deepavali is based on the belief that Lakshmi, the goddess of wealth, will visit homes that are brightly lit up. Indian Americans put up holiday lights and candles and serve festive meals. Many gather at temples for dancing and celebrating as a community.

New Jerseyans gather eagerly to take part in sports and to cheer for their favorite teams. Crowds throng to the Meadowlands to watch football, basketball, and ice hockey. Avid fans support the New York Jets and the Giants of the National Football League (both teams play at the Meadowlands, despite their names), the Nets of the National Basketball Association, and the Devils (named after the Jersey Devil) of the National Hockey League. Baseball fans are not left out, either. Minor league teams include the Trenton Thunder, the Newark Bears, and the Sussex Skyhawks. Many New Jerseyans, particularly in the northern part of the state, support the New York Yankees.

Boxing draws crowds to Atlantic City. Tickets sell quickly for seats at the casinos' hotels, which host championship fights. New Jersey is home to famous boxer Chuck Wepner, nicknamed the Bayonne Bleeder. In 1975, Wepner went fifteen rounds with champion Muhammad Ali in a fight for the world's heavyweight title. His career has been credited as the inspiration for the Rocky movie series.

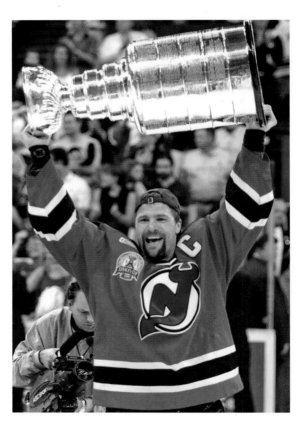

*New Jersey Devils MVP Scott Stevens holds the Stanley Cup after defeating the Dallas Stars in June 2000.*

## NEW JERSEY STATE FAIR

For one magical week in August, New Jerseyans gather at the state fair in Sussex County. A petting zoo delights young children, and dime tosses and dart throws excite others. Plump pigs and brawny bulls are up for inspection, and sleek horses compete at the Sussex County Fair and Horse Show. New Jerseyans have had a long love affair with horseback riding and horse racing.

Incubators lined with baby chicks hatching from eggs remind visitors of the poultry industry that has been part of New Jersey's economy through the years. In celebration of the state's dairy industry, there are cows to be milked.

Lines are long for favorite foods, such as the cheesesteaks and soft pretzels that nearby Philadelphia sends across the Delaware River. "But funnel cake is my weakness," said Stefanie Volkmann of the Greater Cherry Hill Chamber of Commerce. "And I always eat too much!" Dutch farm families invented funnel cake more than two hundred years ago. The Dutch were among New Jersey's first European settlers.

*Monmouth Park Racetrack is one of the world's most beautiful racetracks. It features a 100-foot-wide, 1-mile-long oval track where horses and their jockeys run for the finish line.*

Horseback riding and horse racing are important to New Jerseyans, who claim the horse as their state animal. The United States Equestrian Team chose Gladstone, New Jersey, as its training center. Riding stables in small towns throughout the state offer riding lessons and host horse shows. "When I was eleven, I rode a horse named Chocolate in a horse show at the Woodedge Stables and I won the blue ribbon," said Beverly Tadeu, a forty-year-old woman who continues to ride horses for pleasure. "That day still stands out in my mind as one of the most exciting days of my life." Racetracks throughout the state offer fans the thrill of watching harness and thoroughbred racing.

Recreational sports are also popular. Boating, swimming, and saltwater fishing in the Atlantic Ocean and Barnegat Bay are favorites on summer weekends. Inland, New Jerseyans spend time canoeing and fishing in fresh-water lakes and streams. Hot air ballooning and plane gliding are becoming more and more popular, especially in the northwestern region of the state. Endless nature trails in New Jersey's many state parks lure hikers and bicyclists in spring, summer, and fall, while ski slopes draw crowds throughout the winter. No matter what the season, New Jerseyans enjoy the outdoors.

## Chapter Four

# Rules and Roles

Every state in the country is ruled by its constitution, which acts as the supreme source of state law. New Jersey has had three constitutions over the years. Its third and present constitution was adopted in 1947.

## INSIDE GOVERNMENT

New Jersey's laws are created, carried out, and interpreted by the legislative, executive, and judicial branches of government.

### Executive Branch

New Jersey is one of just two states (the other is Maine) in which the governor is the only executive official elected by the people. The governor appoints the attorney general, the secretary of state, the state treasurer, and the heads of major state departments. All of the governor's appointments must be approved by the state senate. The governor serves as commander in chief of the state's militia and proposes the budget to the legislature.

New Jersey's governor is elected to a four-year term and may serve a maximum of two terms. On January 17, 2006, Jon Corzine took office as New Jersey's fifty-fourth governor. Corzine is a former marine and

*The capitol in Trenton features brilliant stained-glass windows and portraits of the state's early governors.*

*Jon Corzine was elected governor in January 2006. During his campaign, he promised to set a new course for New Jersey.*

investment banker who got involved in politics when he was elected to the U.S. Senate in 2000. When he announced his governorship in 2005, Corzine promised to revamp New Jersey's state property tax system, to build a stronger economy, and to improve education and health care.

Christine Todd Whitman is a notable past governor of New Jersey. In 1993, she became the first woman to be elected governor of New Jersey. She was reelected in 1997. In January 2001, Whitman took office as head of the Environmental Protection Agency under the administration of President George W. Bush.

## Legislative Branch

New Jersey's legislature is made up of a forty-member senate and an eighty-member general assembly. Senators generally serve for four years, but if

*Christine Todd Whitman is one of New Jersey's best-known former governors.*

their term begins with a new decade, it is only two years long. Members of the assembly serve two-year terms. A bill may be introduced in either the senate or the general assembly. Once a bill is passed, it goes to the governor, who either signs it into law, returns it to the legislature with suggestions for change, or vetoes (rejects) it. If two-thirds of both the senate and the general assembly vote to override the governor's veto, the bill becomes law.

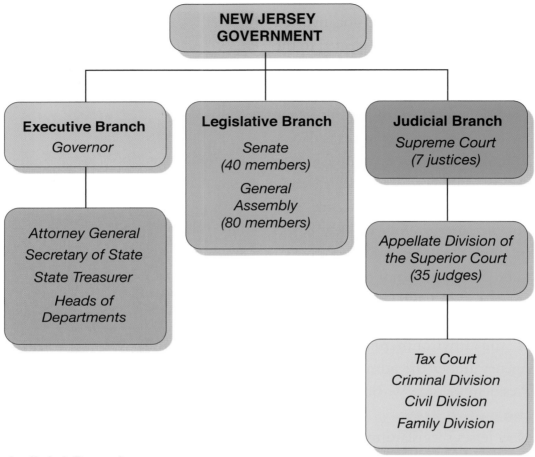

```
                    ┌─────────────────────┐
                    │    NEW JERSEY       │
                    │    GOVERNMENT       │
                    └─────────────────────┘
```

**NEW JERSEY GOVERNMENT**

**Executive Branch**
*Governor*

*Attorney General*
*Secretary of State*
*State Treasurer*
*Heads of Departments*

**Legislative Branch**
*Senate*
*(40 members)*

*General Assembly*
*(80 members)*

**Judicial Branch**
*Supreme Court*
*(7 justices)*

*Appellate Division of the Superior Court*
*(35 judges)*

*Tax Court*
*Criminal Division*
*Civil Division*
*Family Division*

**Judicial Branch**

New Jersey's highest court, the supreme court, is made up of one chief justice and six associate justices. The supreme court hears cases involving constitutional issues and capital punishment. It has the power to overturn decisions made in lower courts, and its decisions are final. The state's chief trial court, the superior court, deals with criminal and civil cases and reviews decisions that have been made in lower courts. New Jersey is one of just four states that still have a chancery court. This court handles cases concerning families.

Members of both the supreme court and the superior courts are appointed to seven-year terms by the governor, with the senate's approval. Judges who are reappointed once are allowed to serve until they are seventy years old.

## LAWS FOR YOUNG PEOPLE

New Jersey has a history of enacting laws to protect children, from required bicycle helmets and seat belts to strict rules for day-care and adoption centers. The state's residents and government officials work hard to ensure that their students receive the best education possible.

Students who are not proficient in English are entitled to receive a bilingual education. In a Spanish-speaking community, for example, teachers are able to speak both English and Spanish with their students. "When we came here from Cuba, the teachers at my school talked to me in Spanish at first and then added English later," said Miguel Fuentes of Union City. "With the teachers using my language, it made me feel more comfortable. It made me feel like I could fit in, and it gave me a chance to do well in school. My grades were good right from the beginning. At home, my family kept on speaking Spanish—only Spanish."

Some people believe that only English should be spoken in American schools. They believe that teaching in multiple languages discourages young immigrants from entering their new culture completely. Bilingual education is debated hotly in New Jersey—and in many other states.

In cases of divorce or when both parents are not living with their children, New Jersey has strict child-support laws. If the parent who is supposed to pay child support fails to do so, the state can withhold money from that parent's paycheck. "My brother and I live with my mom," said a thirteen-year-old from New Brunswick. "Even though my mom works, my

# NEW JERSEY
# BY COUNTY

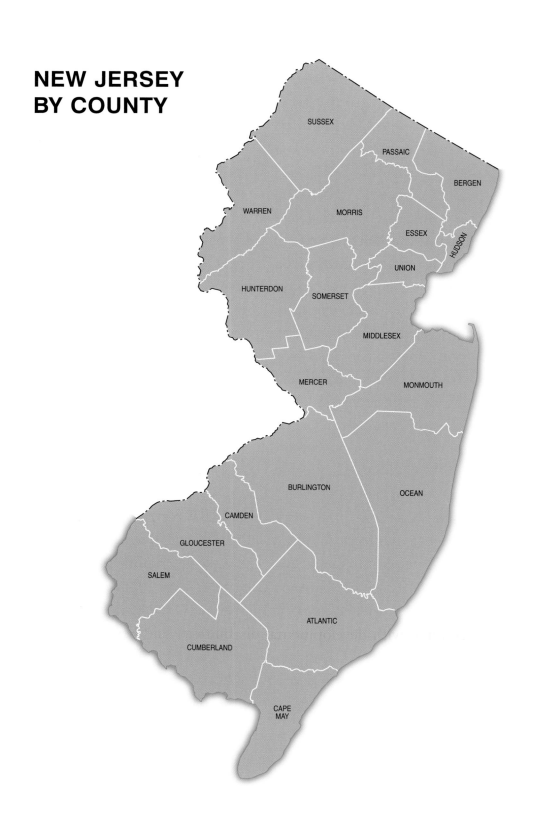

SUSSEX

PASSAIC

BERGEN

WARREN

MORRIS

ESSEX

HUDSON

UNION

HUNTERDON

SOMERSET

MIDDLESEX

MERCER

MONMOUTH

BURLINGTON

OCEAN

CAMDEN

GLOUCESTER

SALEM

ATLANTIC

CUMBERLAND

CAPE
MAY

dad has to pay child support for us. I take art lessons after school and my brother plays on a soccer team, and the child support money helps pay for these things."

In September 2007, Governor Jon Corzine signed a package of seven bills aimed at helping the state's children. Each of the bills related to the disorder of autism. Autism, a developmental disability that affects people's social interaction and ability to communicate, occurs in about 1 of 150 American children. In New Jersey, however, that number is quite a bit higher: 1 in 95. "With new studies showing New Jersey with the highest reported autism rates in the country, it is critically important that the state do

*The general assembly chamber boasts the artisanship of many different craftspeople.*

all it can to help the growing number of individuals and families confronting autism spectrum disorders," said general assembly speaker Joseph J. Roberts. "For families whose loved ones are locked in the grasp of this disorder, today's action sends a reassuring message of hope that New Jersey is working to do more to improve its safety net of services and care."

One of the seven bills set up a program for evaluating infants and toddlers for signs of autism and ensured that they will be referred to health care professionals for early intervention. "Early intervention has performed miracles for children with developmental disabilities," said Senator Loretta Weinberg, a sponsor of the bill. Another bill established an autism awareness training course for emergency responders so that they will know exactly how to handle situations involving autistic people.

## Chapter Five

# An Economic Tapestry

New Jersey has many different types of businesses, which combine to create a strong and diverse economy. The state draws its economic strength from three main sources. First, New Jersey has an excellent transportation system and large ports, which make it easy to receive raw materials and to ship finished goods. Second, the state has a large and well-trained group of workers. Third, New York City, Philadelphia, and other nearby cities provide a solid market for New Jersey's products.

## SERVICES AND MORE

A large majority of New Jersey's economy is made up of service industries. Prudential, the largest insurance company in the United States, is based in Newark. Bell Laboratories, located in Murray Hill, is one of the world's foremost private research complexes. Thousands of New Jerseyans work on life-changing inventions and developments there.

Tourism is a leading service industry. Vacationers flock to New Jersey's seashore, lakes, and parks during the summer. In the winter, ski slopes in the northern part of the state attract crowds. Throughout the year, Atlantic City

*The Port of New York and New Jersey is the largest port on the east coast of North America. Many cargo ships come and go every day throughout the year.*

**77**

lures tourists to its boardwalk—complete with games, amusement rides, and food. In 1976, voters agreed to allow gambling casinos in Atlantic City, and the first casino opened in 1978. Casinos continue to attract huge numbers of visitors who bring money into the state. Today, Atlantic City is one of New Jersey's largest visitor destinations.

Government services, such as military bases, are also important in New Jersey. McGuire Air Force Base, Fort Dix, and the Naval Air Warfare Center at Lakehurst all provide jobs for New Jersey residents. The U.S. Coast Guard operates a training center in Cape May.

Manufacturing is the second-largest part of New Jersey's economy. The state is a leading producer of chemicals and medicines. Four pharmaceutical giants—Bristol-Myers Squibb, Johnson & Johnson, Merck, and Warner-Lambert—have large plants in New Jersey. Food products, machinery, electronic equipment, and printed material are also manufactured in the state.

## 2006 GROSS STATE PRODUCT: $453.2 Million

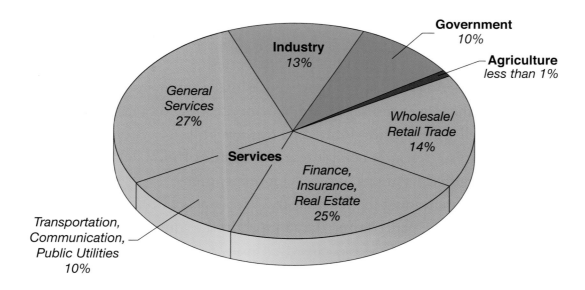

Government 10%

Industry 13%

Agriculture less than 1%

General Services 27%

Wholesale/ Retail Trade 14%

Services

Finance, Insurance, Real Estate 25%

Transportation, Communication, Public Utilities 10%

*At Fort Dix, British explosive ordnance disposal specialists train with American soldiers.*

Even though New Jersey's official nickname is the Garden State, agriculture accounts for less than one percent of its gross state product. Greenhouse and nursery products, such as flowers and shrubs, are the state's most valuable sources of farm income and are grown mostly in the northwest. This region is also home to many dairy farms. The southwestern part of the state boasts farm-fresh apples, peaches, tomatoes, peppers, and corn, while the Pinelands is known for its blueberries and cranberries. New Jersey is one of the nation's top five producers of blueberries, peaches, eggplants, and cranberries.

*Roadside farmer's markets selling tomatoes are familiar summer sights in Hunterdon County.*

New Jersey's coastal waters teem with fish and shellfish. Fishers pull in flounder, sea bass, whiting, crabs, and oysters. The big catch, however, is clams. Two-thirds of the nation's clam harvest comes from New Jersey.

Industrial research and development has been central to New Jersey's economy since Edison set up his research facility in Menlo Park over a century ago. For many years, New Jersey companies produced color televisions and then videotape recorders. Today, its main industries focus on telecommunications, information technologies, and biotechnology.

# NEW JERSEY WORKFORCE

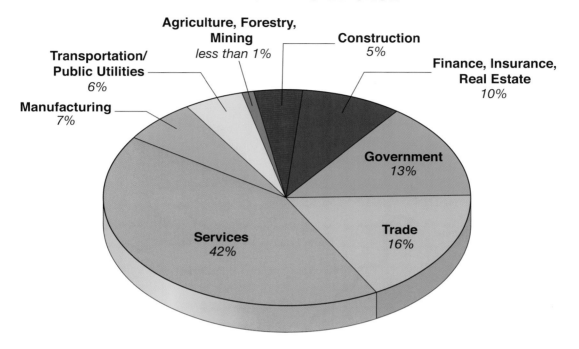

Agriculture, Forestry, Mining
less than 1%

Construction
5%

Transportation/ Public Utilities
6%

Finance, Insurance, Real Estate
10%

Manufacturing
7%

Government
13%

Services
42%

Trade
16%

## NEW JERSEY IN THE GLOBAL ECONOMY

Exports and imports have helped stabilize New Jersey's economy in recent years. In 2006, exports soared to $27 billion—a 28-percent gain over the previous year. In the same year, chemical products made up about one-third of the state's exports. New Jersey also sells computer electronics, transportation equipment, machines, and scrap materials. Steady imports also keep the state's ports busy. In 2006, New Jersey's ports handled 57 percent more cargo than in 2005. This kept people employed in ware-housing, manufacturing, and distribution jobs.

The majority of New Jersey's exports go to Canada, which receives approximately 21 percent of the state's total exports each year. The United Kingdom and Japan receive the second- and third-largest amounts of goods

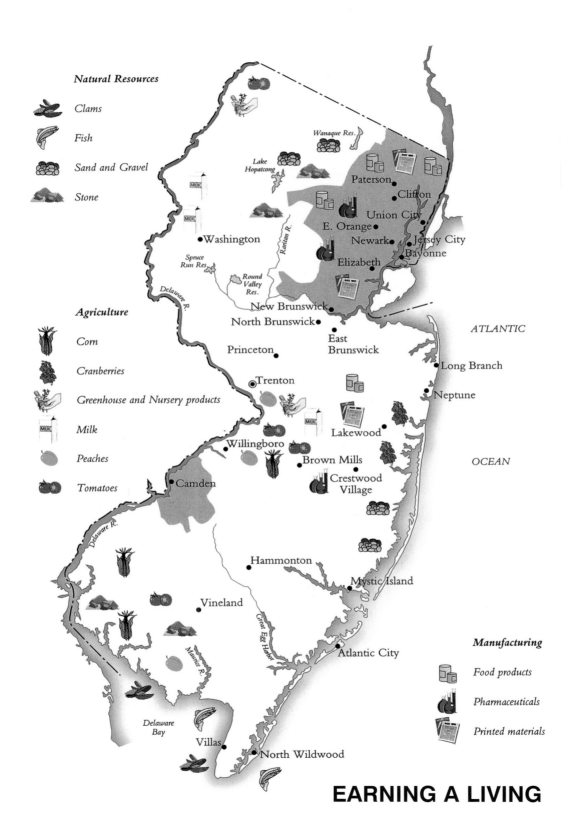

**Natural Resources**

Clams

Fish

Sand and Gravel

Stone

**Agriculture**

Corn

Cranberries

Greenhouse and Nursery products

Milk

Peaches

Tomatoes

Wanaque Res.

Lake Hopatcong

Paterson

Clifton

Union City

E. Orange

Newark

Jersey City

Elizabeth

Bayonne

Rantan R.

Spruce Run Res.

Round Valley Res.

New Brunswick

North Brunswick

Delaware R.

Washington

ATLANTIC

East Brunswick

Princeton

Long Branch

Trenton

Neptune

Lakewood

Willingboro

Brown Mills

OCEAN

Camden

Crestwood Village

Delaware R.

Hammonton

Mystic Island

Vineland

Maurice R.

Great Egg Harbor

Atlantic City

**Manufacturing**

Food products

Pharmaceuticals

Printed materials

Delaware Bay

Villas

North Wildwood

# EARNING A LIVING

exported from New Jersey. Exports to Finland grew 530 percent between 2002 and 2006. New Jersey is still working to balance its trade, as the state imports more goods from around the world than it sends back out.

## COPING WITH HARD TIMES

New Jersey has seen its share of hard times. Camden was hit particularly hard in the late 1980s and early 1990s, when the two largest employers in the city, the Campbell Soup Company and General Electric, made major changes. Although Campbell's headquarters stayed in Camden, it moved its enormous soup-manufacturing operation out of state. "It's still hard for me to talk about it," said Marna Robinson, who made soup for Campbell's for more than thirty years. "My whole life was Campbell's. The people I worked with and me, we were just like family and we loved our jobs. And then, boom!, the bottom dropped out. I work at a sandwich shop now, and it's just not the same."

Shortly thereafter, Campbell's next-door neighbor, General Electric, cut more than three thousand workers, many of whom were electrical and aerospace engineers. "There were so many of us all looking for the same kind of work in the same vicinity that it was almost impossible to find a job in the field," said Dan Davis, an aerospace engineer. "I ended up working as a cashier in a variety store for almost two years before I finally found the engineering job I have now."

In the mid-1900s, telephone giant AT&T, located in Basking Ridge, also cut its workforce. Thousands of employees lost their jobs. Some were rehired after several months. Others were forced to learn new skills and begin new careers. Although New Jersey's workers have had to cope with some dramatic changes, most have found a way to pull through.

## Chapter Six

# A Garden State Tour

Every region in New Jersey is filled with fascinating places. The state has as much to offer its own residents as it does visitors from around the world.

## NORTHERN NEW JERSEY

Liberty State Park, which overlooks the Statue of Liberty, is located in Jersey City. Visitors can travel by ferry to see the giant statue on Ellis Island, where millions of immigrants first set foot on American soil. Back on the mainland, the Liberty Science Center is filled with hands-on exhibits.

The Afro-American Historical Society Museum is also in Jersey City. Exhibits cover a full range of African-American history and culture, from the civil rights movement to African sculpture and musical instruments. There is even a fascinating display of black dolls. The African Art Museum in Tenafly, a little farther north, exhibits African masks, statues, crafts, and textiles.

Also in the state's northeastern corner is Newark, New Jersey's largest city. Amid Newark's tall buildings and bustling streets is Branch Brook Park,

*Visitors to New Jersey find many ways to have fun. Here, a roller coaster thrills passengers at Wildwood.*

*The Infection Connection exhibit draws visitors to the Liberty Science Center, which was renovated and reopened in July 2007.*

which has more than two thousand cherry trees. Hundreds of thousands of visitors gather to admire the trees during the Cherry Blossom Festival every April. Nearby is the Catholic Basilica of the Sacred Heart, an architectural wonder that took fifty-six years to build. Groundbreaking took place in 1898, but the huge Roman Catholic church was not completed until 1954. The building is noted for its soaring towers, pointed arches, and spectacular stained-glass windows, which are considered some of the most magnificent in the world.

At the Newark Museum, New Jersey's largest museum, antique clocks, rare coins, and early American quilts are some of the treasures on display. The museum's Native-American gallery features costumes, jewelry, and tools.

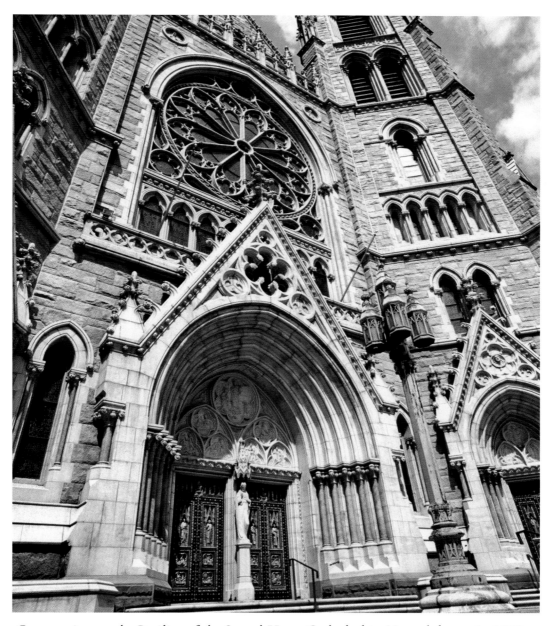

*Construction on the Basilica of the Sacred Heart Cathedral in Newark began in 1899 and ended in 1954.*

Morristown National Historic Park preserves the site where George Washington and his troops spent the winter of 1779 to 1780. While Washington stayed at the comfortable home of Mrs. Jacob Ford Jr., his men stayed 4 miles away at Jockey Hollow. The troops chopped down acres of surrounding forest to build huts for shelter from the coldest winter in a century. As one snowstorm after another prevented food supplies from reaching them, the men came near starvation. Tempe Wick, a young girl who lived nearby, is said to have feared that the starving soldiers would eat her horse, so she hid him in her bedroom for safety. Today, the park includes the Ford Mansion and the Wick House, where visitors can see the little bedroom in which Wick hid her horse. A few log huts have been reconstructed to show how the soldiers lived during that terrible winter.

*These reconstructed soldiers' quarters at Morristown National Historic Park are like the ones that housed the Continental Army during the harsh winter of 1779 to 1780.*

*Thomas Edison's home in West Orange has been declared a National Historic Site.*

The laboratories where Thomas Edison made his great inventions are located in Menlo Park and West Orange. The Thomas Edison Memorial Tower (shaped like a lightbulb on top) and Museum in Menlo Park mark the spot where Edison invented the phonograph and perfected the electric light. In West Orange, Edison's mansion, called Glenmont, and the laboratory where he developed moving pictures have been preserved at the Edison National Historic Site.

Teterboro Airport is home to the Aviation Hall of Fame and Museum of New Jersey. Bronze plaques honor Charles Lindbergh, Buzz Aldrin, and other New Jerseyans who have made aviation history. Aircraft, jet engines, and rocket engines are on display.

## TEN LARGEST CITIES

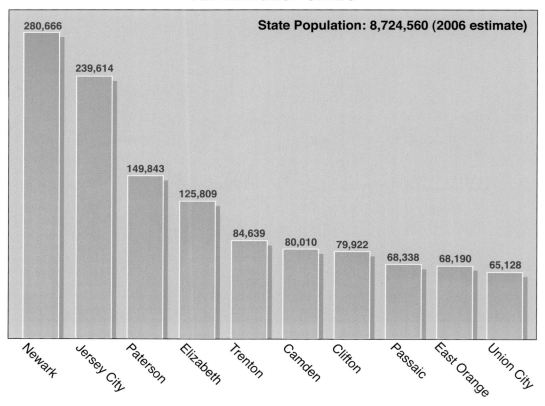

State Population: 8,724,560 (2006 estimate)

- Newark: 280,666
- Jersey City: 239,614
- Paterson: 149,843
- Elizabeth: 125,809
- Trenton: 84,639
- Camden: 80,010
- Clifton: 79,922
- Passaic: 68,338
- East Orange: 68,190
- Union City: 65,128

## CENTRAL NEW JERSEY

The state capitol in Trenton is the second-oldest capitol in continuous use in the United States. New Jersey lawmakers have been meeting there since 1792. Visitors today admire its dome, which is covered in 23-karat gold leaf.

The New Jersey State Museum in Trenton is notable for its display of New Jersey–made pottery and glass. Another impressive exhibit is *Hadrosaurus foulkii*, the first dinosaur skeleton found in the United States.

In 1838, a farmer in Haddonfield came upon some very large bones while digging on his land. He did not know they were dinosaur bones. Twenty years later, when he met a scientist and told him about the bones, he finally found out how great his discovery had been. The scientist wasted no time in having the remaining bones dug up. Over the years, scientists have learned that this creature had a birdlike jaw and walked on its hind legs while using its front legs to search for food. Its posture resembled that of a modern bird. Today, a plaque at the site where the bones were found honors the farmer's fabulous discovery.

In Camden, the Thomas H. Kean New Jersey State Aquarium gives visitors a chance to examine underwater life, ranging from sea turtles to some freaky-looking fish. "I even got to pet a baby shark," said ten-year-old Erin Schonewolf. "Its skin felt just like sandpaper!"

New Jersey is home to Princeton University, the fourth-oldest college in the United States. Founded in 1746, Princeton has educated hundreds of famous politicians, business leaders, artists, and Nobel Prize winners. In 2001, Shirley Tilghman became the first woman president of the university. Princeton is one of the most respected schools in the country.

*Blair Arch is a graceful example of Gothic architecture on the Princeton University campus.*

Rutgers, which was chartered as Queen's College in 1766, is the second-oldest university in New Jersey. The New Brunswick campus is home to the Rutgers Geology Museum, which features fossils and the skeleton of a mastodon, an extinct giant mammal similar to an elephant.

Allaire Village, in Monmouth County, was an ironworks where pots, kettles, and the pipes for New York City's waterworks were made in the early 1800s. Tourists can visit the restored Historic Allaire Village and marvel at the huge beehive-shaped stack that belonged to the original furnace.

The Howell Living History Farm in Titusville gives visitors a chance to see what farm life was like in New Jersey when the twentieth century began. Visitors can watch horse-drawn haying, harvesting, cultivating, maple sugaring, and sheep shearing. Historic Longstreet Farm in Holmdel also gives visitors a chance to look back in time. Farmhands milk cows by hand and use old-fashioned combines to work the fields. They also dress in the style of the late 1800s.

Farther south, in Jackson, the Six Flags Great Adventure Park offers exciting rides and games. A nearby wildlife park has a drive-through safari. Lions, tigers, zebras, baboons, and ostriches are just some of the wildlife living there. The ostriches walk right up to the cars and peck on the windows, and some baboons are so bold that they ride on the roofs!

*At the Howell Living History Farm, visitors can step back in time and see what farming was like many years ago.*

*Riders scream with excitement on Six Flags Great Adventure's Kingda Ka roller coaster, the world's tallest and fastest ride. It goes from 0 to 128 miles per hour in only 3.5 seconds.*

Southern New Jersey is filled with history. For example, the first log cabin built in the United States, the Nothnagle Log House, is in Gibbstown. It was constructed by Swedish settlers in the mid-1600s.

Batsto Iron Works in the Pinelands was a hub of the bog iron industry from the 1760s to the 1830s. During the Revolutionary War, cannonballs and other munitions were made there. Later, the glassmaking industry took hold, but eventually Batsto was abandoned and left to deteriorate. In 1954, the state purchased the land and began to restore the village. Today, small wooden houses are lined up side by side just as they were over a century ago, when ironworkers and glassworkers lived in them. The houses contrast sharply with the grand mansion where the owner lived. Visitors can also visit a general store and a craft and pottery house and imagine what life was like in this forested village long ago.

The Bridgeton area boasts New Jersey's largest historic district. It includes more than two thousand historic homes, churches, and public buildings dating back to the 1700s and 1800s. The Nail House Museum was once part of a thriving nail factory. Today, the building houses a display of antique toys, dolls, and glass and pottery made in New Jersey. Nearby is the Woodruff Indian Museum, which showcases thousands of Native-American artifacts. At the Nanticoke Lenape Village, wigwams and a ceremonial longhouse have been re-created.

*Batsto Village offers visitors an up-close look at an earlier time and a completely different way of life.*

In Millville, where glassmaking has prospered since the early 1800s, visitors can tour the Wheaton Arts and Cultural Center. Many years ago, skilled craftsmen did the fragile work of glassmaking by hand, but today, machines do most of the work. A re-created factory at the center features glassblowers at work. They make lovely vases, pitchers, and paperweights. At the Museum of American Glass, the wondrous displays include old medicine bottles, paperweights, baby bottles, fruit jars, and ink wells.

Rodeo lovers do not have to leave New Jersey to experience the thrill of the real thing. The Cowtown Rodeo, the oldest and largest rodeo on the East Coast, takes place in Woodstown, near Salem, from May to September.

*Vases, pitchers, plates, and cups are displayed at the Museum of American Glass in Millville.*

*The Cowtown Rodeo in Woodstown provides the East Coast with a taste of the wild West.*

In the 1920s, Woodstown was the site of a county fair and auction. Stony Harris, the auctioneer, thought it would be fun to hold a rodeo, and the idea caught on. Today, some of the best cowboys and cowgirls from around the country dazzle spectators with bronco riding, bull riding, and calf roping.

## COASTAL NEW JERSEY

The Sandy Hook Lighthouse was first lit in 1764. This white, 103-foot-tall, eight-sided National Historic Landmark was built because many ships met with disaster while trying to enter New York Harbor. Sandy Hook Lighthouse is the oldest lighthouse in continuous use in the United States.

Also at Sandy Hook is Fort Hancock, which was completed in 1895. For many years, the U.S. Army used the fort to defend New York Harbor. Today, it houses a museum that displays military artifacts and old photographs.

## OLD BARNEY

Among New Jersey's most famous landmarks is the red and white Barnegat Lighthouse, nicknamed Old Barney, which stands at the mouth of Barnegat Inlet. Old Barney began service in 1859 after replacing a 40-foot brick tower. The lighthouse warned passing ships of dangerous shoals until its retirement in 1927, when a lightship anchored 8 miles offshore took over its duties.

Old Barney later served as a lookout tower for the U.S. Coast Guard during World War II. After the war, the state took over the lighthouse and eventually turned the site into Barnegat Lighthouse State Park.

Standing 165 feet tall, Old Barney is the second-tallest of New Jersey's lighthouses. It is also one of the most photographed lighthouses in the country. Visitors may climb 217 steps to the top for a spectacular view of Long Beach Island, Barnegat Bay, and the Atlantic Ocean.

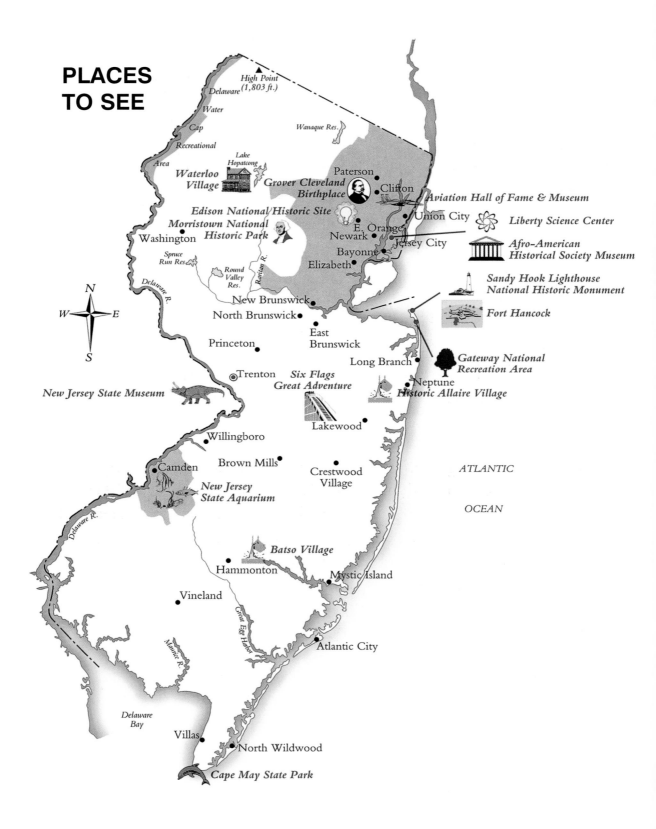

# PLACES TO SEE

High Point
(1,803 ft.)
Delaware
Water
Cap
Recreational
Area
Waterloo Village
Lake Hopatcong
Wanaque Res.
Grover Cleveland Birthplace
Paterson
Clifton
Aviation Hall of Fame & Museum
Edison National Historic Site
Morristown National Historic Park
Union City
Liberty Science Center
Washington
E. Orange
Newark
Jersey City
Afro-American Historical Society Museum
Spruce Run Res.
Round Valley Res.
Bayonne
Elizabeth
Raritan R.
Delaware R.
Sandy Hook Lighthouse National Historic Monument
New Brunswick
Fort Hancock
North Brunswick
East Brunswick
N
W        E
S
Princeton
Long Branch
Gateway National Recreation Area
Trenton
Six Flags Great Adventure
Neptune
Historic Allaire Village
New Jersey State Museum
Lakewood
ATLANTIC
Willingboro
Brown Mills
Crestwood Village
OCEAN
Camden
New Jersey State Aquarium
Delaware R.
Batso Village
Hammonton
Mystic Island
Vineland
Great Egg Harbor
Maurice R.
Atlantic City
Delaware Bay
Villas
North Wildwood
Cape May State Park

At the Gateway National Recreation Area at Sandy Hook, visitors enjoy swimming and canoeing as well as nature walks through a natural holly forest. The forest is the oldest and largest of its kind on the East Coast.

While many visitors to the Jersey shore take in historic sites, they spend most of their time simply relaxing on the beach and swimming in the ocean. Long Branch became famous as the favorite vacation spot of U.S. presidents from the 1860s to the early 1900s. It features a beach called Seven Presidents Oceanfront Park, which honors the presidents who visited there. The town still lures vacationers with its cool summer breezes and refreshing ocean waves.

In the 1860s, Ocean Grove also began to lure vacationers, and by the 1890s, thousands of people flocked to the seaside resort each summer. In 1875, a huge wooden auditorium was built there. Ocean Grove is still popular with vacationers, who enjoy the concerts held in the Great Auditorium.

Lucy, the Margate Elephant, was an unusual attraction when she was built in Margate in 1881. Lucy is 65 feet tall and was originally made of wood covered with tin. Over the years, she has withstood storms, fire, and a short move. In the 1970s, she was restored and given a new steel frame. Lucy has served as a real-estate office, a tourist attraction, a house, and finally, a museum. In 1977, she was made a National Historic Landmark. Visitors can climb the stairs in her hind legs to tour a small museum in her belly, then climb onto an observation deck for a fine view of the surrounding area. "I remember my parents driving us down the shore to see Lucy when I was a little girl," said Lori Knopf, a Delaware resident. "And now here I am with my children!"

*Lucy the Margate Elephant is the oldest example of animal architecture left in the United States.*

Atlantic City, New Jersey's most popular resort, offers something for everyone, from swimming in the ocean to strolling the boardwalk to gambling in the casinos. The world's first boardwalk was laid at Atlantic City in 1870. Jacob Keim, a hotel owner, and Alexander Boardman, a train conductor, came up with the idea of a boardwalk to prevent visitors from tracking sand from the beach into hotels and train cars. The first saltwater taffy was made in Atlantic City in the 1880s. When Charles Darrow sold the rights to the popular board game Monopoly to Parker Brothers in the 1930s, the streets in the game were named after the streets in Atlantic City, Darrow's favorite resort.

*The Atlantic City boardwalk lights up brilliantly at night.*

## BIRDS LOVE CAPE MAY

The Cape May area is a bird haven. More than four hundred species of birds have been recorded in this region, which is one of the best bird-watching sites in all of North America.

Cape May Point State Park is the year-round home of many species. It is also a stop for migrating birds that pass through the area. Particularly spectacular is the hawk (below) migration that takes place in autumn. From early September to late November, hundreds of hawks fly through each day. Some of the species sighted are red-shouldered hawks, northern goshawks, and peregrine falcons. Bird lovers from all over the nation gather for the annual Cape May Hawk Watch, a hike through the area in search of hawks.

Cape May, considered the nation's oldest seaside resort, lies at the southernmost tip of New Jersey. In colonial days, New Jerseyans and Philadelphians enjoyed Cape May's beaches and breezes. By the 1840s, the area was luring summer vacationers from all over. During the final decades of the 1800s, ornate mansions were built in Cape May, and many still stand today. The mansions are celebrated in October during Victorian Week, when they are open for touring, and in December during Christmas in Cape May, when carolers dress in nineteenth-century costumes and make the rounds.

*One of the most recognized homes in historic Cape May is the Pink House.*

In the 1600s and 1700s, before Cape May became a seaside resort, it was a whaling town. Cape May whale oil and whalebone were well-known products in the colonies. Although the whaling industry no longer exists in Cape May, many visitors enjoy taking whale-watching cruises. Besides offering a peek at magnificent sea creatures, these excursions provide a view of the beautiful New Jersey coast.

*THE FLAG: The flag, which was adopted in 1896, is a colored version of the seal set against a yellow background.*

*THE SEAL: In the center of the state seal is a shield picturing three plows, which represent agriculture. The horse's head above the shield symbolizes speed, strength, and agriculture. Flanking the shield are goddesses representing liberty and agriculture. The state seal was adopted in 1928.*

# State Survey

**Statehood:** December 18, 1787

**Origin of Name:** Named after the island of Jersey in the English Channel

**Nickname:** Garden State

**Capital:** Trenton

**Motto:** Liberty and Prosperity

**Bird:** Eastern goldfinch

**Flower:** Purple violet

**Tree:** Red oak

**Insect:** Honeybee

**Animal:** Horse

**Fish:** Brook trout

**Colors:** Buff and blue

*Goldfinch*

*Purple violets*

# IN NEW JERSEY

New Jersey has no official state song. The lyrics to this song were written in 1994 by fourth graders at Van Holten Elementary School in Bridgewater under the direction of teachers Carol Forte, Diane Silverster, and Sandy Vitale. It is under consideration for adoption as the state song.

**Folk dance:** Square dance

**Dinosaur:** Hadrosaurus foulkii

**Shell:** Knobbed whelk (commonly known as the conch shell)

**Soil:** Downer soil

## GEOGRAPHY

**Highest Point:** 1,803 feet above sea level, at High Point

**Lowest Point:** sea level along the Atlantic coast

**Area:** 7,790 square miles

**Greatest Distance North to South:** 167 miles

**Greatest Distance East to West:** 88 miles

**Bordering States:** New York to the north and east, Pennsylvania to the west, Delaware to the southwest

**Hottest Recorded Temperature:** 110 °F at Runyon on July 10, 1936

**Coldest Recorded Temperature:** -34 °F at River Vale on January 5, 1904

**Average Annual Precipitation:** 45 inches

**Major Rivers:** Delaware, Great Egg Harbor, Hackensack, Hudson, Maurice, Millstone, Passaic, Raritan

**Major Lakes:** Budd, Culver, Green Pond, Greenwood, Hopatcong, Mohawk, Swartswood

**Trees:** beech, birch, cedar, maple, oak, pitch pine, sassafras, short-leaf pine, sweet gum, yellow poplar

**Wild Plants:** azalea, buttercup, goldenrod, honeysuckle, jack-in-the-pulpit, mountain laurel, purple violet, Queen Anne's lace, rhododendron, Virginia cowslip

**Animals:** bear, deer, fox, mink, muskrat, opossum, otter, rabbit, raccoon, skunk

**Birds:** blue jay, cardinal, chickadee, duck, goldfinch, goose, partridge, pheasant, robin, ruffed grouse, sandpiper, wild turkey

**Fish and Shellfish:** bass, bluefish, clam, crappie, menhaden, oyster, pickerel, pike, salmon, shad, sturgeon, trout, weakfish

**Endangered Animals:** Indiana bat, roseate tern, eastern puma, hawksbill sea turtle, Kemp's ridley sea turtle, leatherback sea turtle, shorthouse sturgeon, dwarf wedgemussel

**Endangered Plants:** American chaffseed, Knieskern's beaked-rush, sensitive jointvetch, small whorled pogonia, swamp pink

*Hawksbill sea turtle*

# TIMELINE

**1500** The Lenape are living in the area that will become New Jersey.

**1524** Giovanni da Verrazano explores the New Jersey coast.

**1609** Henry Hudson explores the Sandy Hook Bay area.

**1660** Dutch settlers found Bergen, New Jersey's first permanent European settlement.

**1664** The English gain control of New Jersey.

**1666** Newark is founded.

**1746** The College of New Jersey, which later was named Princeton University, is founded.

**1750** New Jersey's first public library is established in Trenton.

**1774** Colonists in Greenwich burn a supply of British tea to protest British taxes.

**1776** George Washington and his troops cross the Delaware River on Christmas night to stage a surprise attack at the Battle of Trenton.

**1787** New Jersey becomes the third state in the Union.

**1790** Trenton is named New Jersey's capital.

**1804** Vice President Aaron Burr kills Alexander Hamilton in a duel at Weehawken.

**1817** The New Jersey state legislature establishes a public school system.

**1858** The first dinosaur skeleton found in North America is discovered in Haddonfield.

**1861–1865** The Civil War is fought.

**1879** Thomas Edison perfects the lightbulb in Menlo Park.

**1884** Grover Cleveland becomes the only native New Jerseyan to be elected president of the United States.

**1912** New Jersey governor Woodrow Wilson is elected president of the United States.

**1919** The first regularly scheduled air passenger service in the United States begins between Atlantic City and New York City.

**1937** The German airship *Hindenburg* explodes over Lakehurst, and thirty-six people die.

**1947** New Jersey adopts its present constitution; the transistor is developed at Bell Labs in Murray Hill.

**1952** The New Jersey Turnpike opens.

**1967** Civil disturbances in Newark leave twenty-six people dead and more than a thousand injured.

**1978** Casino gambling begins in Atlantic City.

**1994** Christine Todd Whitman becomes New Jersey's first female governor.

**1998** The U.S. Supreme Court rules that most of Ellis Island comes under the jurisdiction of New Jersey.

**1999** Hurricane Floyd causes major flood damage.

**2001** Former New Jersey governor Christine Whitman becomes the head of the Environmental Protection Agency under the administration of President George W. Bush; almost seven hundred New Jerseyans are killed in a terrorist attack on September 11.

**2005** The U.S. Department of Defense announces the closing of Fort Monmouth, which will take effect no later than September 15, 2011; New Jersey becomes the first state to award public funding for stem cell research.

**2007** New Jersey recognizes civil unions of same-sex couples.

## ECONOMY

**Agricultural Products:** beans, blueberries, corn, cranberries, greenhouse and nursery plants, milk, peaches, potatoes, soybeans, tomatoes

**Natural Resources:** clams, clay, crushed stone, fish, sand and gravel

**Manufactured Products:** chemicals, electrical equipment, food products, machinery, pharmaceuticals, printed materials, scientific instruments

**Business and Trade:** insurance, real estate, research laboratories, transportation, wholesale and retail trade

*In Hackensack, "Robby" the robotic pharmacist finds prescriptions for the store's customers. New Jersey is a leader in the pharmaceutical industry.*

**Super Science Weekend** Each January, the New Jersey State Museum in Trenton sponsors a celebration of science and technology. Visitors can take part in science experiments, watch special planetarium shows, and hear scientists talk about their work.

**Cherry Blossom Festival** A half million people visit Newark's Branch Brook Park each April to admire the spectacular blossoms of the park's 2,700 cherry trees.

**Shad Festival** Each April, Lambertville celebrates the shad that migrate up the Delaware River. Thousands of people come to enjoy such fish dishes as shad cakes, shad gumbo, smoked shad, and shad salad. The event also features storytelling, music, and a dance.

**Whitesbog Blueberry Festival** A running race through the Pinelands kicks off this June event in Browns Mills. Afterward, children make crafts, play games, and go on a hayride. Popular snacks include blueberry muffins, pies, and pastries, but the festival favorites are blueberry sundaes, made with creamy vanilla ice cream and topped with gooey blueberry sauce.

**Hungarian Festival** Hungarian Americans of New Brunswick honor their ancestors at this June festival. In addition to tasting all kinds of Hungarian food, you can enjoy Hungarian folk music and dancers and admire Hungarian art.

**New Jersey Seafood Festival** Each June, seafood lovers descend on Belmar to devour lobsters, clams, crabs, oysters, shrimp, and fish cooked every way imaginable. Besides all the food, there are crab races, model boat competitions, music, and an arts-and-crafts fair.

**Polka Spree by the Sea** For four days each June, the island resort of Wildwood kicks up its heels as bands on the boardwalk provide the music for twelve hours of nonstop polka dancing each day.

**Hambletonian Day** The premier harness race in the United States takes place in East Rutherford each August. Spectators watch magnificent horses race around the track. Kids take pony rides and enjoy the performances of clowns, jugglers, and musicians.

**Festival of the Sea** The highlight of this September event at Point Pleasant Beach is an inner-tube race in the ocean. Those who would rather stay on land can eat seafood, listen to music, and watch a spectacular fireworks display.

**Wings 'n' Water Festival** Stone Harbor celebrates southern New Jersey's coastal habitat with this September event. The festival features environmental exhibits and workshops, displays by wildlife artists, salt-marsh safaris, and a seafood feast.

**Scandinavian Fest** People from throughout North America descend on Waterloo Village in Stanhope each September to perform the music of Norway, Iceland, Denmark, Finland, and Sweden. Visitors stroll among crafts exhibits and attend music workshops.

**Chatsworth Cranberry Festival** Cranberries are everywhere at this October event in Chatsworth. You can taste cranberry cakes, pies, relishes, jellies, pancakes, and honey. There are also contests for the best cranberry-decorated hat and the most cranberry-colored car. Even the festival's flower arrangements and artwork must include cranberries. You can top off your day by touring a cranberry bog.

**Christmas Candlelight House Tours** In December, you can travel back in time and get in the holiday spirit by touring two dozen of Cape May's quaint nineteenth-century homes and churches, all decked out in their holiday best.

**Reenactment of Washington Crossing the Delaware** Each December, thousands of history buffs gather in Trenton to reenact George Washington's historic crossing of the Delaware River on Christmas night.

## STATE STARS

**William "Bud" Abbott** (1896–1974), who was born in Asbury Park, was half of the wildly popular comedy team Abbott and Costello. In such fast-talking routines as "Who's on First?" the tall, thin Abbott played straight man to the chubby, excitable Lou Costello.

**Charles Addams** (1912–1988) was a cartoonist who first became famous for drawing morbid, spooky cartoons for the *New Yorker* magazine in the 1930s. He is best remembered for creating the comically ghoulish Addams Family. These characters were the basis of a television series in the 1960s and two popular movies in the 1990s. Addams was born in Westfield.

*Reenactment of George Washington crossing the Delaware River, Christmas Day*

**Edwin "Buzz" Aldrin** (1930–   ), of Montclair, is a famous astronaut. In 1966, he became the third person to leave a spacecraft and "walk" in space. His was by far the longest and most successful spacewalk up to that time. Then, in 1969, Aldrin followed Neil Armstrong out of *Apollo 11* to become the second person to set foot on the Moon.

**Amiri Baraka** (1934–   ) is an influential poet and playwright who writes about the plight of African Americans. In the 1960s, Baraka advocated black separatism. His 1964 award-winning play, *Dutchman*, was a landmark in African-American theater. In the 1970s, Baraka rejected black separatism when he became a communist. Baraka was born Everett LeRoi Jones in Newark. He changed his name when he converted to Islam.

**Willaim "Count" Basie** (1904–1984), a native of Red Bank, led one of the greatest jazz bands of all time. As a child, Basie played drums before turning to piano. He performed in other people's groups until he founded his own band in 1935. Basie's group became one of the leading bands of the swing era. Basie continued to lead his own orchestra into the 1980s.

**Judy Blume** (1938–   ), who was born in Elizabeth, writes books for young people and adults. Her writing is known for its wit, honesty, and compassion. She first came to prominence in 1970 with her novel *Are You There God? It's Me, Margaret.* Her other notable books include *Superfudge, Tales of a Fourth Grade Nothing,* and *Tiger Eyes.*

*Willaim "Count" Basie*

**William Brennan** (1906–1997), who was born in Newark, was a justice on the New Jersey Supreme Court before being appointed to the U.S. Supreme Court in 1956. During his thirty-four years on the court, Brennan proved himself a solid defender of freedom of speech, freedom of religion, and other liberties.

**Aaron Burr** (1756–1836), of Newark, was a U.S. vice president who killed his longtime political rival Alexander Hamilton in a duel. This event ended Burr's political career. Later he was involved in a scheme to invade Spanish territory in the Southwest. He was tried for treason but acquitted.

**Grover Cleveland** (1837–1908) was the twenty-second and the twenty-fourth president of the United States. He was the only native New Jerseyan to become president, the only president elected to two nonconsecutive terms, and the only president to get married while in office. Cleveland was born in Caldwell.

**Lou Costello** (1906–1959) was half of the most popular comedy team of the 1940s. He and Bud Abbott were renowned for their fast-talking, carefully timed patter. They made many successful movies, including *In the Navy* and *Abbott and Costello Meet Frankenstein*. Costello was born in Paterson.

**Stephen Crane** (1871–1900) was a poet and novelist known for his brutally honest and pessimistic vision of life. Crane, who was born in Newark, began his career as a newspaper reporter covering the slums of New York. His own poverty and his work as a journalist served as the

*Grover Cleveland*

basis of his first novel, *Maggie, a Girl of the Streets*. He is most famous for his novel *The Red Badge of Courage*, a psychological study of a young Civil War soldier.

**Thomas Edison** (1847–1931), perhaps the world's most famous inventor, spent most of his adult life in New Jersey. Edison was born in Milan, Ohio. He became a telegraph operator in 1862. Two years later, he created his first invention, an automatic telegraph repeater. He eventually moved to the East Coast, and in 1876 he set up an invention factory in Menlo Park, New Jersey. Edison hired chemists, physicists, and mathematicians to help him solve problems. He later moved his research laboratory to West Orange. Edison's greatest accomplishments include perfecting the lightbulb and developing the phonograph and the motion picture.

**Allen Ginsburg** (1926–1997), a poet, was the leading spokesman of the beat generation, whose writers rejected the constraints and conformity of the 1950s. Ginsburg first gained prominence in 1956 with his poem "Howl," a long, angry cry of despair that criticizes conventional society and social ills. Ginsberg's poetry is characterized by vivid images and graphic language. He was born in Newark.

**Whitney Houston** (1963– ), of Newark, is among the most popular American singers in history. Her first album, *Whitney Houston*, hit number one on the pop charts in 1985, and the song "Saving All My Love for You" earned her a Grammy Award. Her second album, *Whitney*, was also a smash, and she became the first popular singer to sell 10 million copies of each of her first two records. Houston is also a successful actress. She appeared in such hits as *The Bodyguard* and *Waiting to Exhale*.

*Thomas Edison*

**Carl Lewis** (1961–   ) is one of the greatest track and field athletes of all time and the winner of nine Olympic gold medals. In 1984, he became the second person in history to win four gold medals at a summer Olympics. After winning four straight gold medals in the long jump from 1984 to 1996, he became the second person to win the same event in four consecutive Olympics. Lewis was born in Birmingham, Alabama, and grew up in Willingboro, New Jersey.

**Jerry Lewis** (1926–   ), a popular comedy actor of the 1950s and 1960s, was born in Newark. Early in his career, Lewis was part of a comedy team with Dean Martin. Beginning with *My Friend Irma* in 1949, the duo made seventeen movies in which Lewis played hysterical, clumsy characters opposite Dean Martin's suave ladies' man. After the team broke up, Lewis directed and starred in his own films, such as *The Nutty Professor*. Today, he is perhaps best known for hosting the annual Jerry Lewis Telethon for Muscular Dystrophy, which has raised hundreds of millions of dollars to fight the disease.

**John McPhee** (1931–   ), the author of more than twenty nonfiction books, is known for being able to make any subject interesting and for giving a balanced perspective on conflicting viewpoints. McPhee was born in Princeton and attended Princeton University. He had already written several books when he finally gained prominence in 1977 with the best seller *Coming into the Country*, a book about Alaska. Although McPhee has written about subjects as varied as sports and travel, most of his writing has been about nature. *The Pine Barrens* is a book about his native state.

*Carl Lewis*

**Jack Nicholson** (1937–   ) is a leading film actor famous for his menacing grin and eccentric characters. Nicholson first drew attention in 1969 for his role as a lawyer who drops out of conventional society in *Easy Rider*. A string of great roles in such films as *One Flew Over the Cuckoo's Nest*, *Five Easy Pieces*, *Chinatown*, and *The Shining* made Nicholson famous. He has earned three Academy Awards, most recently for the 1997 film *As Good As It Gets*. Nicholson was born in Neptune.

**Dorothy Parker** (1893–1967) was a poet, short-story writer, and critic known for her dark, biting humor and elegant satire. Early in her career, Parker was a critic for the magazine *Vanity Fair*, but she was fired because she often wrote devastating reviews of major plays. She then moved to the *New Yorker*, where she stayed until her first poetry collection, *Enough Rope*, was published and became a best seller. In the 1920s and 1930s, Parker was a member of the Algonquin Round Table, a group of writers who hung out at New York City's Algonquin Hotel and became famous for their witty conversation. Parker was born in West End, a part of Long Branch.

**Alice Stokes Paul** (1885–1977) was a women's suffragist who grew up in Mt. Laurel. While studying in England, she became involved with the movement to gain the vote for women, which she continued upon her return to the United States. She wrote the Equal Rights Amendment and fought for the equality of women worldwide.

**Paul Robeson** (1898–1976) was a singer famous for his deep, rich voice. Robeson was born in Princeton and attended Rutgers University, where he became the first black all-American football

*Jack Nicholson*

player and won first prize in the college's speaking competition four years in a row. After graduating from Columbia University Law School, Robeson joined a New York law firm, but his career was cut short. He then turned to performing. He appeared in such works as *Othello* and *Show Boat* and became one of the first African Americans to play serious roles. Robeson was also politically active; he fought for black rights around the world. His association with the Soviet Union eventually brought criticism from the U.S. government, and his career declined sharply in the early 1950s.

**Ruth St. Denis** (1879–1968), one of the founders of modern dance in the United States, was born Ruth Dennis in Newark. In St. Denis's day, the only types of dance performed in the United States were ballet and vaudeville. In 1906, St. Denis appeared in her own work, *Radha*, which was based upon dances of India. Throughout her career, she incorporated many Asian influences and stressed individuality and expressive movements. In 1915, St. Denis cofounded the influential Denishawn Dance School. For many years this school was the training ground of every important American dancer and choreographer.

**Antonin Scalia** (1936–    ), a Supreme Court justice, was born in Trenton. Scalia was a law professor and an official in the U.S. Justice Department before being appointed to the U.S. Court of Appeals in 1982. Since being named to the Supreme Court in 1986, he has become known for his sharp intellect and his strict conservatism.

*Antonin Scalia*

**Norman Schwarzkopf** (1934–   ) is a retired U.S. Army general who planned and executed the United States–led attack on Iraq during the Persian Gulf War. Schwarzkopf, whose father was a general in World War I and head of the New Jersey State Police, attended the U.S. Military Academy at West Point, served in Vietnam, and then rose through the ranks to become a general. He was born in Trenton.

**Frank Sinatra** (1915–1998) is one of the most popular singers in U.S. history. Sinatra, who was born in Hoboken, began singing in clubs as a teenager. With his relaxed, resonant style, he became one of the best-known singers of the big band era. He was a darker, more melancholy figure in the 1950s, when he sang about loneliness and last chances. Sinatra also acted in movies. He earned an Academy Award for playing a feisty soldier in *From Here to Eternity*. Sinatra continued performing into his eighties.

**Bruce Springsteen** (1949–   ) is a popular rock-and-roll performer who grew up in Freehold and began his career in Asbury Park. Beginning in the 1970s, he became the voice of working-class New Jersey, as he sang about dead-end jobs and young people searching for freedom. Springsteen became a superstar in 1984, when his album *Born in the U.S.A.* sold 20 million copies and stayed in the top ten for two years.

**Alfred Stieglitz** (1864–1946) was a photographer and gallery director who led the movement to get photography recognized as an art. Stieglitz began entering his photographs in competitions in the 1880s, and he won over 150 awards. Although at first he photographed picturesque scenes, his images became more abstract as he used lines and shapes to

*Bruce Springsteen*

convey emotion. His 291 Gallery in New York became the leading promoter of modern art in the United States. It displayed works by modernists such as Pablo Picasso. Stieglitz was born in Hoboken.

**Meryl Streep** (1949–    ) is one of the country's best film actresses, known for her ability to disappear into any role. She was a well-respected stage actress before she made her screen debut in the 1977 film *Julia*. Throughout her career, she has given one stunning performance after another in such films as *Sophie's Choice* and *Silkwood*. Streep has been nominated for fourteen Academy Awards and has won twice. Streep was born in Summit.

**John Travolta** (1954–    ) is a popular movie actor with good-humored charisma. In the 1970s, Travolta became a teen idol for his role as a dim-witted high school student in the television comedy *Welcome Back, Kotter*. He soon appeared in a string of hit films, including *Grease* and *Saturday Night Fever*. In the 1980s, Travolta had a few good roles and then fell into obscurity. His career was rejuvenated in 1994, however, when he earned an Oscar nomination for his role as an amiable hit man in *Pulp Fiction*. Today, he is again one of the nation's leading actors.

**Sarah Vaughan** (1924–1990), who was born in Newark, was one of the world's best jazz vocalists. Her career took off after she won the Apollo Theater's Amateur Night contest in Harlem in 1942 and was invited to join Earl Hines's band. During her long career, she was praised for her rich voice, amazing range, and improvisational ability.

*Sarah Vaughan*

**Selman Waksman** (1888–1973) was a scientist who discovered several medicines, called antibiotics, that saved countless lives. Waksman was born in Ukraine and moved to the United States in 1910 to attend Rutgers University in New Brunswick. He eventually became a professor at Rutgers, where he did research on antibiotics. His discoveries enabled doctors to cure many infectious diseases, including tuberculosis. Waksman was awarded the Nobel Prize in medicine in 1952.

**Christine Todd Whitman** (1946–    ) is the first female governor of New Jersey. Whitman was born in New York but grew up in Old- wick, New Jersey, where her parents were prominent members of the Republican Party. After narrowly losing a race for the U.S. Senate in 1990, Whitman was elected governor in 1993 and reelected in 1997.

**William Carlos Williams** (1883–1963) was a writer of poems, novels, short stories, and other genres. He was interested in both everyday subjects and romance. Williams grew up in Rutherford and returned there after he earned a medical degree. He spent forty years working as a doctor and writing poetry during his spare time. One of his most famous works is a long poem called *Paterson*.

## TOUR THE STATE

**Franklin Mineral Museum** (Franklin) This museum houses the world's largest collection of fluorescent minerals, which were found nearby. It also includes a replica of a zinc mine just like the one where miners found the amazing Franklin rocks.

**Great Falls Historic Landmark District** (Paterson) Smack in the middle of Paterson, you can visit the 77-foot-high Great Falls of the Passaic River. You can also see some of the mills that the falls powered.

**Liberty Science Center** (Jersey City) This hands-on museum has rotating exhibits involving all branches of science.

**Newark Museum** (Newark) A planetarium, a sculpture garden, and an important collection of Native-American art are all part of this diverse museum.

**Sandy Hook Lighthouse** (Highlands) The oldest operating lighthouse in the United States, the Sandy Hook Lighthouse has been warning ships since 1764.

**Edison National Historic Site** (West Orange) While visiting Edison's laboratory, you'll see a demonstration of his phonograph and watch *The Great Train Robbery*, an early motion picture filmed with Edison's equipment.

**New Jersey State Aquarium** (Camden) At this vast aquarium, you can touch a shark, admire a coral reef, and put on a helmet that lets you listen to dolphins communicating with one another.

**Lucy, the Margate Elephant** (Margate City) Climb the stairs inside this six-story-high elephant for a nice view from her back. Lucy was built in 1881.

**Barnegat Bay Decoy and Baymen's Museum** (Tuckerton) This museum celebrates the sea culture that once thrived on Barnegat Bay. You can learn all about boatbuilding, clamming, and oystering and admire many beautiful, hand-carved wildfowl decoys.

**Black River & Western Railroad** (Flemington) Take an 11-mile ride on a vintage steam-powered train through the farmland of western New Jersey.

**Delaware and Raritan Canal State Park** (Stockton) This 70-mile-long park along an old canal is the perfect place to hike, bike, ride horses, and fish. It also contains seventeen historic buildings to explore.

**Morristown National Historic Park** (Morristown) This park preserves the area where the Continental army spent the brutal winter of 1779 to 1780. The site includes a museum housing eighteenth-century weapons and George Washington memorabilia. You can also visit the mansion where Washington spent the winter and see replicas of log huts where the soldiers lived.

**Six Flags Great Adventure and Wild Safari** (Jackson) Enjoy amusement-park rides at Great Adventure and see more than 1,200 animals, including zebras, bison, and giraffes, at the separate wildlife preserve. As you drive through the park, animals might come right up to your window.

**Batsto Village** (Hammonton) This preserved village re-creates life in the Pine Barrens of the nineteenth century. At the site, you'll learn about the early iron-making industry and see what life was like for the people who worked there.

*Siberian tiger at Great Adventure and Wild Safari, Jackson*

**Wharton State Forest** (Hammonton) This forest is an ideal place for outdoors enthusiasts to hike, camp, fish, and canoe in the mysterious Pine Barrens.

**Edwin B. Forsythe National Wildlife Refuge** (Oceanville) A huge variety of birds spends part of the year at this refuge. Species include peregrine falcons, piping plovers, and snowy egrets.

**Historic Cold Spring Village** (Cape May) You can see craftspeople demonstrating such skills as spinning and weaving at this re-creation of a nineteenth-century village. You can also visit an old railroad depot, a school, and a jail.

**Cape May Point State Park** (Cape May) Bird-watchers flock to this park to glimpse hawks and other migrating birds. Sometimes they also see dolphins from the beach.

**Wetlands Institute** (Stone Harbor) The institute is filled with displays and hands-on exhibits about the wetlands of southern New Jersey. Visitors can also climb a tower that provides a fabulous view of the surrounding area or walk on a trail that leads out into a salt marsh.

## FUN FACTS

New Jersey boasts a few firsts when it comes to sports. The first professional basketball game was played in Trenton in 1896. The first college football game was played in New Brunswick in 1869. Princeton played Rutgers, and Rutgers won.

The world's first drive-in movie theater opened on June 6, 1933, outside Camden. It had room for five hundred cars.

Atlantic City has the longest boardwalk in the world.

The world's tallest water tower is in New Jersey.

Rutgers University hosts a cockroach derby each year.

# Find Out More

If you would like to find out more about New Jersey, look in your school library, local library, bookstore, or video store. You can also surf the Internet. Here are some resources to help you begin your search.

## BOOKS

Dalton, Anne. *The Lenape of Pennsylvania, New Jersey, Delaware, Wisconsin, and Ontario*. New York: PowerKids Press, 2005.

Martinelli, Patricia and Charles A. Stansfield Jr. *Haunted New Jersey: Ghosts and Strange Phenomena of the Garden State*. Mechanicsburg, PA: Stackpole Books, 2004.

Moran, Mark. *Weird N.J.: Your Travel Guide to New Jersey's Local Legends and Best Kept Secrets*. New York: Sterling, 2006.

Orr, Tamra. *A Primary Source History of the Colony of New Jersey*. New York: Rosen, 2005.

## WEB SITES

**State of New Jersey**
www.state.nj.us/
Find information about arts and recreation, education, and New Jersey history. Information about the state's most exciting sites and attractions can also be found.

**New Jersey Division of Travel and Tourism**

www.state.nj.us/travel/

Learn about tourist attractions, outdoor activities, athletic events, and other ways to spend time in New Jersey.

**NJ.com: Everything Jersey**

www.nj.com

Read local and national news, learn about events and entertainment, and participate in forums about life in New Jersey.

**The New Jersey Historical Society**

www.jerseyhistory.org

At this site, you can read about exhibits on various aspects of New Jersey history.

# Index

Page numbers in **boldface** are illustrations and charts.

Wendy Moragne is a freelance writer who enjoys teaching young people through her writing. She has lived in New Jersey most of her life.

Tamra B. Orr is the author of more than one hundred nonfiction books for people of all ages. She wishes she had as much time to read as she does to write and keeps collecting books for when that day comes. Orr writes testing materials and test-preparation books for various standardized tests. She is mom to four charming kids and partner to one charming husband.